The Lived Religion

ISBN 979-8-9935291-0-3 (Paperback)
ISBN 979-8-9935291-5-8 (Hardcover)
ISBN 979-8-9935291-3-4 (Kindle E-book)
ISBN 979-8-9935291-4-1 (EPUB E-book)
ISBN 979-8-9935291-1-0 (Digital Online)
ISBN 979-8-9935291-2-7 (Audiobook)

www.TheLivedReligion.com

Contents

The Lived Religion - An Interpretation

Chapter 1

1 With Kodesh Scriptures, no matter how pure the original inspiration poured out from the Divine Ruach-ual Fountainhead, they still have to pass through fallible human hands,

2 and this could lead to differences of interpretation and discord among the readers, things most undesirable, where harmony and unity are to be the rule,

3 to avoid all such differences, and for the sake of accord and unity, the interpretation of Kodesh Writings should be restricted to conform with the following rules:

4 The interpretation must accord with authentic traditions,

5 it must accord with reason and experience, faith never contending with reason,

6 though it is realised and acknowledged that the nature of life, being as it is, many things have to be accepted and undertaken without logical explanations:

7 The continuance of life beyond the veil of death may not appear to accord with worldly experience and reason,

8 for the benefit of man there is a Mishpat prohibiting any assurance of this,

9 that life does, and other such things, have to be accepted on faith,

10 therefore, worldly experience cannot be taken as the yardstick

in this instance, as in many other instances;

11 apart from worldly experiences, there are Ruach-ual experiences, and these can only be known and understood by the one having endured them,

12 what is told of these to others must be accepted on faith.

Chapter 2

1 Whenever there is a meeting among brothers, they should assemble in good order, with goodwill and harmony in their hearts, they should likewise disperse!

2 while things are done in this manner there will be prosperity and progress,

3 they will remain while the teachings are esteemed and the doctrines hallowed,

4 while the leaders are held worthy of loyalty, and the brothers of comradeship;

5 progress and prosperity will not depart while the brothers are upright and steadfast,

6 while the maiden sisters are modest and virtuous, and the married sisters are decent and decorous,

7 while the elder brothers are wise and diligent in preserving all that is good,

8 while the elder sisters are careful in all they do, and considerate for the welfare of the younger ones;

9 it is for the old to keep watch and ward, and for the young to dare and do;

10 the harshness of the Mishpatim should be mitigated with loving kindness,

11 and when brothers or sisters are seen to be falling into the ways of wickedness, they should first be warned,

12 let some able and discreet person take them in hand and counsel them,

13 after being warned, they should be reminded, and only after this should they be disciplined;

14 these teachings are always right:

15 Those which teach the proper channelling of the desires and urges of the body, not those which would pander to them or ignore them,

16 those which place Ruach-ual objectives above worldly things,

17 and those which uphold the virtues and principles of humanity, and attack anything which would bring them down!

18 when any disagree as to a teaching, each shall converse with the other with friendliness, self-control, and reason, following at all times the road of common sense!

19 frugality is not meanness, prudence is not fear,

20 wastefulness is not generosity, weakness is not kindness,

21 happiness is not pleasure, apathy is not shalom,

22 the defence of principles is not intolerance, idealism is not prejudice,

23 to compromise is not to surrender,

24 to defer to the wishes of a loved one is not weakness of character,

25 to avoid argument and discord within the family requires strength, while assertion displays inconsideration,

26 they who stifle hasty or thoughtless words are better than they who speak according to their thoughts,

27 to stand up for your rights is not necessarily right, and to do all things for shalom and harmony is often wrong, the way of goodness traverses a very narrow ledge!

28 the man who says, "Perhaps I am wrong" is always right, the man who says, "I am certainly right" is always wrong,

29 to avoid a fight is not cowardice, to fight with the certainty of victory is not courage,

30 weak men may often fight and strong men often run, motive is all that matters,

31 to judge anyone by his actions alone is to judge unfairly.

Chapter 3

1 Scriptures come in many tongues, they serve different purposes and vary in value,

2 but each suits and serves a group of people in a particular stage

of ruach-ual development,

3 the lessons of an infant are as essential to its future as are the lessons of an older child,

4 each Scripture gives a glimpse of the light, a Ruach-ual revelation from a different viewpoint,

5 but in each case the light is the same,

6 for there is only one light of Truth!

7 however, Divine Writings need interpretation, for they conceal more than they reveal, and they are never just what they appear to be on the surface,

8 if a particular Scripture proclaimed that fire actually gives out cold instead of heat and that the sun really sheds darkness instead of light, the shallow-minded person would turn from it in scorn,

9 but this irresponsible and thoughtless attitude cannot be applied to Kodesh Words,

10 and it would be much wiser to assume that the Scripture intended to convey a meaning and message quite different from the superficially apparent one,

11 Divine Scripture cannot be treated like entertaining and valueless literature! therefore, delve deeply and diligently!

12 the only conclusion an intelligent person can come to is that all Kodesh Scriptures, read properly and really understood, originate at One Source,

13 and, reveal only a fraction of the whole on the surface, and so,

14 in worldly matters,

15 in rules of life, and code of conduct and morals,

16 in all things governing life on Earth,

17 they will be interpreted strictly, according to their obvious meaning and intent;

18 in all things pertaining to Ruach-ual matters,

19 the afterlife,

20 the Divinity,

21 or not strictly concerned with earthly life and existence,

22 they need not necessarily be interpreted literally, for writing as an earthly medium is inadequate to express such things concisely.

The Lived Religion - Book 1 - The Voice of Elohim

Chapter 1

1 I am established in glory! I am The Self-Formed One! I am The Glorious One! I am The Victorious One!

2 all is in Me, and I am in all! I can span ten thousand lands or dwell within the heart of a mote,

3 there is no here and yonder, the far is near and the near far,

4 there is about Me an infinitely vast expanse of unmoulded space wherewith to labour, and this is a place of unending toil and gratification, I stand on the strand of a formless sea,

5 earthly words are unavailing for expression and lead to falsity and confusion! it is like trying to pour the Nile through a straw,

6 I am the Voice of Elohim, Who is the Adonai of All Men and Ruler of Men's Hearts!

7 I have many aspects and come differently to all men, I am the Elohim of Many Faces!

8 to you, My servants, I give these words, that they may be carried to all men:

9 Obey My Torot, and I will be your Elohim,

10 I will enlighten and instruct you, guiding you along the way,

11 I desire your love and loyalty, and your adherence to My Plans, but I do not desire your servility,

12 I am not only your Elohim, but your Commander as well, and so I expect obedience and discipline, as befits those who prepare for harsh and grim battles, such as those which lie ahead,

13 My desire is for love, rather than futile sacrifices of burnt offerings,

14 but it should not be a passive love, but one expressing service in My Cause,

15 a certain knowledge of right and wrong, with free choice of the former, is of greater value in My sight than pointless ritualistic worship,

16 I derive no pleasure from the wasteful shedding of blood from bulls and lambs,

17 I gain nothing from the fat of sheep and the flesh of goats,

18 I am the Creator of All, so what can men give that would increase My greatness? selah;

19 men are misled if they believe that their sins can be purged by vain rituals! only active goodness can obliterate the stain of sin!

20 men approach Me in fear, they come to Me with servility, they beg forgiveness for their sins, and request My help in worldly matters,

21 to sing My praises is their excuse for coming into places made Kodesh unto Me,

22 but they come wanting something, be it only reassurance,

23 with this attitude towards Me, do you wonder that I remain mute before their pleas?

24 bring Me no more vain offerings of flesh and blood! for such wastefulness of life is an offence to the Adon of Life!

25 men themselves may derive benefit from these, but their hypocrisy when they proclaim they do this in My Name is not hidden from Me,

26 give Me dedication and effort, that is all I ask,

27 and above all be true to yourselves, for I abhor the face of hypocrisy, the face now all too familiar when men approach Me,

28 men bring Me meat and wine, fine flour and wheaten cakes, thinking I can consume these, or that I have need of such sustenance,

29 I would be far better served were these to be given to the widow and orphan, to the multitudinous poor whom you suffer to exist in your midst!

30 poverty is man-made, and it is not sufficient for the wealthy to give alms to the poor,

31 those with power and position, with wealth and plenty, must strike at the roots of poverty,

32 if they fail to do this, then the alms they give have no merit in My sight;

33 the reek of your incense smoke rises and disappears into the air, but it comes not unto Me, nor do I have need of it,

34 yet, I will not deny you the pleasure of its fragrance, which can bring inner harmony and shalom by soothing the ruchot of men,

35 nor will I deny you your hags, if the fetters of wickedness be thereby loosened from your souls, but do not say they are undertaken for My benefit or glorification!

36 fasting and the denial of bodily appetites may serve useful ends for men, but though you may deceive yourselves regarding their intent, do not try to deceive Me by misstating their purpose,

37 I have no desire to repress the joy and exuberance welling up in the hearts of men! far rather would I prefer that such humanising emotions be cultivated!

38 therefore, pray if prayer serves its true purpose, which is to harmonise your ruach with Mine,

39 keep your moadim and hags if they serve their purpose, which is to inspire and refine your ruach,

40 do all that elevates your ruach and develops your soul! that is the true purpose of life,

41 do all that is good for you, nothing wholly beneficial is denied you, but do not declare that in so doing you confer benefit upon Me! I am the Elohim Above and Beyond All!

Chapter 2

1 If a man seeks to enter My presence by prayer, and says, "Adonai, grant me this or give me that," the thing will be neither granted nor given unless it be for his ruach-ual good or benefit another,

2 I am no huckster bargaining blessings in exchange for worship,

3 nothing man can give can add to what I have,

4 also men do Me little honour when they fail to recognise that I am above concern for mere bodies, which decay and fall apart when the ruach leaves them,

5 yet, man is but man, know that I am an Elohim of understanding and compassion,

6 if man cries out to Me, in genuine stress and suffering, he will not go unrelieved and uncomforted, but have you not understanding that suffering and sorrow are for the benefit of men?

7 I do not deny you your rituals and ceremonials, worship Me as you will, but bear in mind that this cannot substitute for your obligations,

8 ritual and worship cannot be an adjustment or payment for the things you have failed to do, or be an apology for your own shortcomings, neither do they compensate for iniquities against your fellow men,

9 if you attach importance to ritual and ceremonial, let it be in a proper proportion, and never let them dull your conscience against deeds of wickedness, of usury, and injustice!

10 never let your duty and obligations be neglected because you worship Me diligently!

11 let this not become an excuse for failing to share your bread with the hungry, or for neglecting the needs of the destitute or weak, I am not deceived,

12 a life dedicated to Me is not one preoccupied with worship, that is more the life of a coward trembling before the unknown,

13 he who dedicates his life to Me gives shelter to the homeless and succours those in distress, but even these are not the ultimate in goodness, for they are passively accepted,

14 the ultimate in goodness is to actively combat all the root causes of evil!

15 those who are My true followers live a life of service and goodness, they live in harmony with their neighbours, harm none, and do not shirk the burdens and obligations of earthly existence,

16 Earth is Earth, take it as you find it, do not expect to find Heavenly things there,

17 it is a place of tuition, and the purpose of life is learning,

18 all things of Earth are limited and mortal, immortality will not be found there,

19 when the things of Earth have fulfilled their purposes, each passes away, returning to the dust from whence it came;

20 to listen to the words of the Kodesh Writings while striving to understand them is better in My sight than offerings of flesh and treasure, which benefit the priests more than they do Me,

21 I am better served by obedience to My Torah and conformity with My Plan.

Chapter 3

1 Among the things which I abhor, few are more detestable than the hypocritical offerings of the evildoer,

2 behold, the offerings and worship of a hypocrite are an

abomination to Me!

3 evil enters the realm beyond Earth as a foul smell, and the worse one of all is the smell of hypocrisy,

4 moreover, those who pander to hypocrites, or do not actively oppose them, are also creatures of evil!

5 I know too well the deceit to which men are prone: The adulterer and fornicator preach chastity for others, while the liar declares the virtues of Truth,

6 the thief preaches honesty, and the lewd-minded professes modesty, men say one thing and mean another!

7 men may deceive themselves and other men, but I am not deceived,

8 now I say, let men first cleanse their own souls, and eradicate hypocrisy, before presuming to approach Me!

9 men may well cry out, "Why does Elohim remain mute? why has He deserted me?" do they think their deeds are hidden? or that I cannot read the secrets of their hearts?

10 worship by men of iniquity is mere mockery, how rare the sincere and genuine heart!

11 were men indeed deserted by their Elohim, they would have none to blame but themselves,

12 do men think their lack of kindness and consideration for others, their insincerity and inconsistency, are truly hidden from Me? I am The All Knowing One!

13 and I see too little love of goodness in the hearts of men, and

too much fear for the consequences of their deeds,

14 real and sincere worship is to obey My Torah and to shoulder the responsibilities of men, to steadfastly conform to My Plan, and to live in neighbourly harmony;

15 he who devotes his life to Me also devotes it to his own welfare, he who serves Me well likewise serves himself, this is the Torah of Torahs,

16 for the whole purpose of life is not the service of Elohim, but the development of the soul of man!

17 ask yourself what My Torah teaches and what qualities it creates, and then you will know whether it is necessary, does not restraint also lead to greater enjoyment and appreciation?

18 no man can say that the Mishpatim of the Torah really detract from the joys of life, neither can it be said they are obstacles to the gratification of normal desires and the natural craving for pleasure,

19 read and examine them carefully, to what normal desire do they deny gratification? what natural impulse do they attempt to destroy?

20 what reasonable pleasure do they prohibit? and what beneficial outlet do they seek to suppress? selah;

21 I have endowed the creature made in My likeness with a religious instinct, for this springs from its everlasting ruach, as fire generates heat, therefore, to worship is not unnatural,

22 but blind worship lacks the vitalising element, it defeats its own end,

23 for in true worship, man should reach out beyond himself to discover his own soul, then, having done so, he should develop it until the soul aspires to elohim-hood itself!

24 therefore, dedicate all your labours and the skill of your hands unto Me, and let your heart ever dwell on the borders of the ruach-ual,

25 let the life which you cherish be the ruach-life!

26 free yourself from all vain hopes and selfish thoughts, from all worthless encumbrances! from ungainful avarice and unbeneficial lusts, from the domination of the flesh!

27 life is not easy, nor is it wholly pleasant, it is not meant to be, but bear your burdens with cheerfulness and fortitude, entrench yourself within an inner fortress of shalom,

28 whatever you do or give, do or give in My Name and whatsoever sufferings descend upon you, suffer them for Me,

29 thus, you will avoid the stigma of false pride, and all given and suffered will be without any taint of self-interest,

30 the path of elohim-liness is not an easy one to follow! for it is beset with the pitfalls of perplexity and doubt,

31 though the true path is lit by the guiding light of Truth, not all see it alike, but the fault lies not so much in the light as in the beholder,

32 it is this which leads to misunderstandings concerning each other's teachings, and to disputes between those who see things one way and those preferring another,

33 each considers his own way, his own interpretation of the

light, to be the best, if not, the only way!

34 there are few, even among truly enlightened men, who are able to conceive My true nature,

35 and these know that I am even above unchangeability in manifestation: I can think of Myself as some other, and forthwith, that other comes into being,

36 then there are those among men who declare all life, all My creation, to be an illusion of the senses, a dream without sustenance,

37 they are in error, for all that is real and all that exists was ever latent, awaiting the awakening kiss,

38 because men cannot know Reality as it actually is, but only as they can conceive it to be with their deceptive senses, does not make it any less real; if all men were blind, the stars would still exist.

Chapter 4

1 Neither Reality, nor Truth, nor Elohim, will be inconceivable to the mind of the ultimate man,

2 man in his present undeveloped state, and in his ignorance, cannot conceive such things, and therefore because in his blindness they are beyond his sight, he says they do not exist!

3 in the beginning, I established the Torah, without which the souls of men could not develop and progress,

4 as each soul is itself a Divine fragment, with all the powers of Divinity latent within itself, it can modify all but the Torah,

5 man thinks, but his thoughts alone do not create, for as yet, he lacks knowledge of the power which creates in substance;

6 first, I created the matrix of all,

7 then, when I took thought, creative power flowed outward, and, operating upon the medium, brought into being things of substance,

8 My creation arose before Me as light does before a flame or heat before a fire, it came, and still comes into being, because I exist, it is because I Am!

9 creation in no way affects Me any more than a man is affected by his shadow, or light by its reflection,

10 as raindrops, waves, rivers, dew, and mist are all forms of water, so is everything existing and knowable by man but various forms of the one substance,

11 this substance has its origin in Me, but it is not Me,

12 I am the source of all things, supporting, but not being supported by them!

13 even as the mighty winds which sweep across the Earth find their shabbat in the tranquil vastness above, so all beings and all things have their shabbat in Me,

14 it is a power outflowing from Me, which holds all things in stability and form.

Chapter 5

1 They who devote their lives to My service must do more than love and worship Me, for such service entails the elevation of mankind, the spreading of good, and the combating of evil,

2 they must not only fight against the wicked, but also overcome the wickedness welling up in their own thoughts!

3 they who love Me desire the wellbeing of all men, and their soul is filled with harmony and shalom,

4 dearer to Me than their love for Me, is the labour and tribulations of those who serve Me, I am their end,

5 I am never the Adonai of Inertia, but the Adonai of Effort,

6 if you offer no more than deeds done in My service or in conformity with My Design, then you serve Me adequately,

7 however, too rarely do the ways of men conform to My Plan, and the ranks of those who serve are too thin,

8 therefore, I shall call forth leaders from among men, and send out the clarion cry to service!

9 I shall seek out men who will serve Me diligently and loyally, they will be men of goodwill, who are of a friendly nature,

10 they will be kind and compassionate, men who can love deeply and truly, whose steadfastness is the same in pleasure and affliction,

11 whose resolve remains equally unbroken in the sweet embrace of good fortune as under the harsh blows of misfortune;

12 I will send men who are fair and just, proud and determined, but these qualities mean nothing unless they also have courage

and resolution, fortitude and tenacity;

13 I shall seek the man who is himself ever seeking, who seeks to unravel the riddle of life,

14 one whose persistence is stout, who detests wickedness and delights in the good, whose heart and inner vision reach out for enlightenment,

15 his tranquillity will remain unshaken under stress, and within his heart will be a haven of shalom, beyond the reach of excitement and anger,

16 he will be a lover of wisdom and seeker of Truth!

17 he who is wise, he who knows what to do, who remains calm when others lose their self-control, he who is clearheaded under stress, who enjoys the challenge of the task, that man is Mine!

18 he who labours uncomplainingly, who disdains to satisfy deforming lusts, whose ruach remains the same under the temptations of honours or the pressure of disgrace,

19 he who is free from the shackles of unworthy earthly attachments,

20 who retains his balance under praise or blame,

21 who can shoulder his own burdens,

22 whose ruach is calm, silent, and strong under all circumstances,

23 he who can bear the responsibilities of life and the obligations of love, that man is Mine!

24 I am the Elohim of Inspiration! I am the Elohim of Love!

Chapter 6

1 I am The Knower and you are the known, I am The Source of Life!

2 in the vastness of My nature I place the seeds of things to be, from which come forth all things, that are now, or ever will exist!

3 be wise, there is no need to engage in long-winded empty discussions about far away things lying beyond the reach and understanding of men,

4 but, men must nourish their ruach and sustain it with ruach-ual fare, they must also learn that the ruach is not something separate from man or something within him:

5 Man is ruach! man is soul!

6 to know the reality of the ruach and to establish the existence of the soul, man has only to delve within his nature, to seek within himself,

7 the ruach-ual part of man is not a mysterious something outside his being, or a thing difficult to understand, to discover it requires no more than the effort of seeking,

8 men with sincere hearts, seeking a path to Me, ask Me for a starting point: For most, the key is self-discipline,

9 and this is the reason for many Mitsvahs and Mishpatim, but these must never be unnecessarily restrictive, each must have a definite purpose and beneficial end, obscure though these may seem,

10 the means for overcoming unwholesome desires and for harmonising with the Divine Chord lie within the reach of all, but effort must be expended in the cultivation;

11 if the end is great beyond man's conception, it is no less true that the task before man is arduous and difficult in the extreme:

12 To master himself and gain complete self-control, however this is no more than the first step along the path;

13 though men may despair because I am veiled from them, though they may seek without finding, I am not indifferent to their needs and desires,

14 doubt and uncertainty are essential earthly conditions serving a definite end,

15 I have not surrounded men with perplexities and obscurities unnecessarily,

16 the climate of unbelief and materialism, strange though it may seem to men, is best for their ruach-ual health,

17 I know better than men themselves what is best for them, for I alone can see the broad Design spread over the ages, I alone see the end and objective!

18 though unenlightened men expect it, it is not meet for Me to interfere unduly in the affairs of Earth,

19 all things are Mine and under My dominion, but man may deal with them as he will, I do not interfere,

20 but finally, man is accountable! selah;

21 though I have all, and nothing can add to My grandeur, with all this I still labour!

22 therefore, man should never disdain to labour, for this is an attribute of the Highest,

23 I do not require of any man that he do something I would not do, or be something I would not be, I am the El of Righteousness,

24 if ever I ceased to labour, the universe would be without order, chaos would prevail and precede its destruction;

25 I am the Elohim of Many Aspects, for men may conceive Me in any form they wish, or even as something without form,

26 I am the Adonai of Men's Hearts, in whichever way and by whatever name men serve Me, abiding by My Torot, and conforming with the Great Design, is right in My eyes,

27 any path which will bring man to his goal, is the right road,

28 truly the paths chosen by men are many and varied, some are even devious, but if they be true paths of enlightenment and development, they are acceptable in My sight,

29 however, those who lust for earthly power, offering sacrifice and worship to earthly elohim conceived to accord with their desires, are not acceptable to Me!

30 it is true that earthly success and power may come to those who strive for them, but do they achieve anything more than fleeting satisfaction?

31 what manner of being would now dominate Earth, had all men been without Divine enlightenment from the beginning?

32 if earthly ends alone had dominated men's minds?

33 consider what earthly life would have been like, had it been left to develop predominated by materialism,

34 if it had not been mitigated by injections of the Divine.

Chapter 7

1 There are four main types of men who are good and serve Me well:

2 They are those who suffer courageously the afflictions and sorrows which develop the soul,

3 those who labour that Earth and man may benefit,

4 those who seek after Truth,

5 and those with vision and creativity;

6 yet how rare are those among these, who do not besmirch their record with deeds of evil and thoughts of wickedness?

7 all too many may have, by their carnal desires and acts of wickedness, countered their goodness, to the detriment of their immortal souls!

8 if a man follow a false elohim with goodwill and honesty, serving men well and living in accordance with My Torot, I will not repudiate him, and he will not be denied enlightenment on the way,

9 there are many roads along which the soul may travel to bring about its development and awakening to self-consciousness, but is

it not advantageous to choose the best one?

10 only the foolish travel blindly, without seeking guidance and directions,

11 those who have little wisdom or who are easily misled follow roads which go nowhere,

12 they who follow a barren faith reach a barren destination, and they find only an empty place devoid of hope, incapable of fulfilling their dreams and aspirations,

13 those who worship elohim of their imagination, elohim in strange likenesses, which have been brought into being by man's creative conceptions, will go to these elohim, who do have an existence in a dim shadow realm,

14 those who worship lower satans will go to them, and those who worship the demons of darkness will join them, for what a man desires, he deserves!

15 as there is a link between that which men desire, and what becomes established in existence,

16 provision is made for man to receive the fruits of his own creations,

17 whatsoever you do, whatsoever you plan or create, whatsoever you suffer, let it be an offering unto Me, not for My sake, but for yours! selah;

18 I am the Adonai of Compassion, the Elohim of Understanding,

19 from those who in their devotion offer Me but a single leaf, a flower or fruit, or even a little water, this I will gladly accept, thus lightening their loving ruach, for it is offered in sincerity of heart,

20 he who comes before any elohim, whatsoever its image, with pureness of heart and good motives, comes unto Me! for I gaze upon him with compassion and understanding,

21 I am not concerned with the deeds alone of men, but with their motives, empty gestures are ignored, but that which is done with good intent and a loving heart, never goes unheeded.

Chapter 8

1 I am The Hidden One, hidden to serve an end, veiled in mystery I am further obscured by the mists of mortal delusion,

2 unable to see Me, men declare I do not exist! yet I declare to you, that man with his mortal limitations sees only a minute part of the whole,

3 man is the slave of illusion and deception!

4 though man is born to delusion, for it is a needful state, he is further inflicted by deceptions wrought by men;

5 man cannot perceive the greatness above him, because of its greatness, neither can he see the smallness beneath him, because of its smallness; from the greatest came the smallest and from the smallest came creation,

6 and within the smallest is greatness and power, for the smallest is far less than the mote, yet it is the upholder of the universe,

7 and it shines like the sun beyond the darkness!

8 it lies out towards the edge of the reach of man's thought;

9 in the beginning, all things arose from the invisible, and into the invisible all things will disappear in the end, but the end is not the end of the Ruach,

10 out beyond this material creation born of the invisible, there is a higher Eternal invisible of greater substance, when all material things have passed away, this will remain,

11 above all, is Timelessness which is Eternity, and there is My Abode, the supreme goal of man, and those who attain it dwell in Eternity! I am the Eternal Elohim!

12 few are they who can conceive of Me as I really am, The Unborn and Uncreated! Beginningless and Without End! Adonai of All!

13 as thick clouds of smoke rise up and spread out from a fire burning in damp wood, so did the material universe come forth from Me,

14 as a lump of salt dropped into a pool of water dissolves and cannot be removed afterwards, yet from whatever part of the water you draw there is salt, so it is with My pervading Ruach,

15 I am The Great Luminary, the everlasting source of light sparks, which, imprisoned in matter, become the slumbering souls of men,

16 these, unconsciously guided, spread out the senses under the control of unconscious thought,

17 that which the senses harvest departs with the ruach, it is borne away by the ruach, even as perfume is carried by the wind;

18 I am The Boundless One! The One Beyond Limitations, I remain free and unencumbered by the effort of creation,

19 I Am, and I watch life unfold, I set the course which nature follows to bring forth all that lives! selah;

20 the fools on Earth who shut their eyes and complain because they stumble, the ignorant who choose to walk in darkness, and the apathetic who choose paths of ease and comfort, these have no knowledge of Me,

21 their hopes are sterile, theirs is the choice of darkness, theirs the choice of ignorance, theirs the choice of apathetic inertia,

22 their learning is futile, their thoughts fruitless, and their deeds without purpose;

23 though man is born in ignorance and darkness, he is also heir to the guiding light which dispels them, and the light is his for the taking!

24 then there are the awakened souls among men: Their sustenance is My Own nature, they know My Ruach is among men as an everlasting source of strength and refreshment to the weary and disheartened,

25 they are in harmony with My Ruach, and therefore, know Me.

Chapter 9

1 Men call Me the Adonai of Battles, which I am not, for good men fight each other when kings declare war,

2 men call Me many things, but this does not make Me become what they think I am,

3 I am the hidden power which ultimately rights all wrongs!

which will eventually redress all injustices!

4 I come to all who are worthy, but it is the lonely, the unwanted, the undesirable whom I seek,

5 to Me, the dispirited, the perplexed, the sorrowful and humiliated soul is an irresistible magnet;

6 I am the welcoming light at the end of the road, the companion who watches in compassionate silence, the understanding friend, the ever-ready arm, I am He Who presides over the haven of shalom within your heart,

7 I turn a like countenance to all men, My love for them remains constant,

8 but those who join Me in devotion to My Cause are truly in Me and I am in them,

9 this is My everlasting and unchanging promise unto men: He who walks with Me, serving My Cause, shall not perish!

10 so join your ruach with Mine, giving Me your confidence and trust, and thus united in a harmonious relationship, you will come to know the Supreme Elohim!

11 men say they cannot know Me through their senses, and this is true, for I am above and beyond the reach of their finite senses,

12 the senses of man are not meant to be the means for experiencing Me, they are for experiencing the material, they are also limiting, shutting out far more than they reveal,

13 yet men have within them, a greater sense, which can know Me, but this lies dormant in the mass of men,

14 as the sun radiates heat and a lamp light, so does the heart of man create his own ruach-ual state,

15 I am the Adonai of Men's Hearts, The Consciousness of All Living Things!

16 I am the Elohim of Consciousness, The Listener in the Silences!

17 I do not manifest to man through his mortal senses, for these are bounded by earthly limitations,

18 I manifest through the great sense which is of the Ruach, the sense of the soul!

19 as pure light hides many colours, so am I hidden in the hearts of men,

20 as sparks fly from a bellows-blown fire, so from the Eternal Fire, the life sparks fly out to glow for an instant in matter, and then fall back, selah;

21 the eye of man sees a pebble, a star, a sheep or a tree, and these do not appear to him in any way alike, yet all are differing forms manifesting in the one outflowing force originating with Me,

22 this outflowing force generated that which gave birth to substance, and endowed it with the matrix of form,

23 your soul is a fragment of Divine Ruach interpreting that which the Divine Ruach created! selah; but the soul of man cannot know it in its Reality, for enshrouded in matter they sleep,

24 because the material is a separate part of the greater whole, the mortal part of man can never hope to know in full its boundless

beauty, or experience its limitless bliss!

25 out beyond the limits of man's thought and conception, beyond reach of even the most vivid imagination, the wonder and glory of it all stretch out into absolute perfection!

26 even at the outer reaches, where Eternity begins, the wonder of the inner glory remains veiled,

27 no words of man can ever hope to describe the true nature of Divine things, to the Divine alone can the Divine be known,

28 the radiant Living Heart pulsating with love can never be known to man, but when man becomes more than man, he may take his first glimpse behind the veil, I am The Inspiration and Goal of Man!

29 before creation, I was the One Alone, I thought, and the thought became a command of Power, and into the void of the invisible came that which was the potential of substance, though itself then part of the invisible,

30 light was born of the Power, and My Ruach was in the midst of the light, but it was not that light which lightens the day,

31 a matrix became the foundation of all things, matter gradually forming there, becoming ever denser as it thrust outward from the invisible,

32 it moved from a subtle state to something more solid, from intangibility to substance,

33 from incoherent substance into a state of density and form,

34 I commanded the subtle substance, with light but without form, to mate with the subtle substance of darkness and become

dense, it did so and became water,

35 then I spread water over the darkness below the light, placing a fountain of light about the waters,

36 this brought forth the light of mortal vision, which is not the light of the Ruach, nor the light of Power,

37 all things began with the intoning of the first creative sound, this rushed outward like a great wind-borne roar, and creation marked its passage!

38 then, like a great tidal wave falling back towards the sea, it drew back on itself, leaving the least of its substance at the farthest point of penetration,

39 the waters of creation are deepest in the Realm of The Ruach and shallower at the Ruach-ual edge of the Realm of Matter and Mortality, outward from there, they lessen to nothing,

40 at that time, the universe was made, and then Earth received her form,

41 it slept warmly in the midst of the waters, which were not the waters of Earth, and this was before the beginning of life in earthly substance,

42 I am I Am, the Adon of Creation!

Chapter 10

1 At the foundations of My creation are Truth and Reality, these are with Me and of Me, but they are not My substance, neither are they things comprehensible on Earth,

2 these are truly great things indescribable in the inadequate words of men, which can do no more than form an imperfect, incomplete, and distorted picture of them,

3 simple things can be described clearly in a few words to the understanding of man, but greater things become increasingly difficult to deal with through mere words,

4 what words of man can be used to describe the indescribable? how can things beyond the comprehension of mortal men be brought within the limits of their understanding?

5 before the shadow, there was the reflecting light, a light so bright that were it not veiled in the darkness, it would consume the shadow,

6 seeking to explain and describe transcendental things in the limited language of man only leads to obscurity and confusion,

7 the words form incomprehensible sentences, and unthinking men will declare them to be incoherence,

8 therefore, look behind the sentences strung together with mere words, I am the Unknown Adon, veiled from man by man's mortal limitations,

9 the universe came into being and exists because I Am! it is My reflection in matter!

10 as a man remains unaffected by the manifestations of his shadow, so do I remain unaffected by the material creation,

11 as heat comes forth from fire and contains its essence and nature, though it is not fire, neither has it the substance of fire, so does My creation relate to Me;

12 I am as an object reflected in water: The water may not know the reflection or find it within itself, but this inability has no effect on the reality of the object, nor on the fact of its reflection,

13 it is as a man looking into clear water on a calm day sees his reflection therein, but if the wind blows the image becomes distorted, and if the sun hides its face, the image disappears,

14 yet, none of these effects touches upon the image itself, nor upon that which casts the image,

15 when the wind drops, the cloud vanishes, and the sun reappears, both distortion and deception end, and the reality is again reflected;

16 within My creation is My Ruach, which supports it, and this Ruach is the bond between My creation and Myself,

17 no man acknowledges the air when it is still, but when this same air becomes a whirlwind, men give it their whole attention!

18 with Me, all is real, while with man all is illusion, but man may abandon his illusions in seeking Me, and he will thereby discover Reality!

19 I am The Reality Behind the Reflection, I am The Uncaused Cause!

Chapter 11

1 Those who turn away from the glorious jewel within, to seek an outside elohim, a separate, unresponsive being, are looking for a mere trinket, while disregarding the priceless treasure already in their keeping,

2 men of light worship the Creator of light! men of darkness and ignorance worship ghosts and dark ruchot, shades of the night!

3 there are men, who, moved by dark beliefs or their carnal lusts and perverted passions, perform awful austerities and self-mutilations never ordained by Me,

4 they delight in tormenting the life and ruach within their bodies, they are truly deluded victims of the darkest form of ignorance,

5 yet, some derive pleasure from their pains and torments, and so continue them, but these may be truly described as mutilated souls;

6 there are some men that follow elohim who punish wickedness and reward good, and therefore tend towards goodness, but is it not folly to follow non-existent elohim?

7 all men choose their own ruach-ual destiny, whether it be done knowingly or not, for under the Torah their future state must rest in their own hands,

8 I am the Elohim Who ordained the Torah, and nothing man can do will change it!

9 My Love alone mitigates the consequences of man's unredeemed wickedness! selah; I am The Changeless One,

10 could an Elohim of Love become an Elohim of Vengeance?

11 revenge is something alien to Me, therefore, is it reasonable that men should believe I could be one thing today? and then, because they fall into error, become something else tomorrow?

12 My nature is not as that of man, I Am as I Am,

13 I am not influenced by the mere formal actions of men, or by empty sacrifice, lighted lamps and candles, days of fasting and self-mortification by man cannot sway Me in his favour,

14 I am not to be bribed, for I am Elohim,

15 he who handles fire carelessly and gets burnt cannot blame the fire, neither can he who goes into swift waters and drowns blame the waters, there are Torot, the violation of which brings retribution in its train!

16 they, who by their own deeds, bring pain and suffering upon themselves, cannot blame Me for what ensues,

17 these are the effects of violating My Torot, which are easily understood,

18 men bring down calamity and suffering upon their own heads and blame Me! when the fault lies with them, and the cause is their own misconduct or misconception,

19 men reap as they sow and I am The Fertile Field, which takes no part in the sowing or the reaping,

20 man is his own master and the adon of his own destiny,

21 he cannot expect help from any Great Power, unless he himself expend effort to contact such Power, and independently, be deserving of help,

22 everything a man is or becomes is the result of his own striving and efforts, or his lack of them,

23 I made man to be a man, not a mere puppet or nursling! I am the Adon of the Torah! I am the Adonai of the Stalwart!

24 man is the heir to Divinity! and the road to Divinity is ruach-uality,

25 man cannot become ruach-ual except through his own efforts and striving,

26 he cannot achieve it by being led by the hand, or through fear of punishment, nor by greed through anticipation of a reward,

27 he who enters into his heritage of Divinity will be no weakling! he will have trodden a hard and stony path.

Chapter 12

1 Man has two ways of knowing Me: He can know Me through his own ruach-ual awakening, or through the continued revelation of Torah and Divine Purpose by My inspired servants,

2 to know Me through a ruach-ually awakened self is the way of certainty, but few can suffer its austerities and disciplines;

3 when the ruach of man is unawakened, he cannot know the greatness within him, of which he is a part,

4 not knowing his true nature and unable to see clearly, he is blinded by material delusions,

5 would not the creatures of the night which never see the sun, deem the moon to be the most brilliant light in the sky above? so it is with the man walking in the darkness of ruach-ual unconsciousness,

6 he says, "I am the body, and the body is my whole being," and in the delusion of that belief, he becomes ensnared in an existence bound to matter,

7 like the creatures bound to an existence in the night, which cannot know the glories of things flourishing in the brilliance of daylight, so it is with men bound to the darkness of ruach-ual ignorance,

8 as a shadow in the night is mistaken for an intruder, or a mirage is mistaken for a pool of clear water, so does the ruach-ually immature man mistake the material body for the whole living being,

9 as the shimmering heat haze appears like solid water, so does the outer body appear as the whole being to the ruach-ually unawakened,

10 as to a man in a moving boat, another boat lying still on the water will often appear to be moving, while he himself seems to remain still, so the unawakened ruach is deluded by appearances, seeing the mortal body as a whole being,

11 thus it is with the ruach-ually unawakened man, who, in his ignorance, thinks the mortal body is the whole being, and, having no knowledge or experience of the Ruach-ual region, is deceived,

12 in fact, all the beliefs of man which hold that the mortal body is the whole being, are generated in the darkness of ignorance,

13 a man may be wise in the ways of men, but completely ignorant and unaware of the higher, more glorious things which are revealed in the light of the Ruach!

14 the man held in bondage to delusion says, "If there be another me, a part of me of which I am unaware, it cannot be real, neither can I know it,

15 my eyes are infallible guides, seeing things just as they are,

and any feelings I may experience have their origin within my mortal being, I am the child of my body,"

16 this man is deluded! are the eyes which see mirages totally reliable?

17 the deluded man ignores the ruach-ual part of his being and its needs,

18 he cherishes the mortal body, gratifying its desires with earthly pleasures, like the silkworm, he becomes captive in a cocoon of his own making,

19 the man who lavishes undue care on the mortal body displays his own ruach-ual ignorance and inadequacy;

20 to be free from existence in the darkness of ignorance, to know the glory of life in the light of Ruach-ual consciousness, a man must first awaken his ruach! in this way alone can he become aware of his true nature:

21 Ask yourselves, "What am I? what is real within myself? what comprises the whole man?

22 can it be that I am truly no more than this fleshy thing?

23 the petty, immature, unstable being balanced between futile unearthly ideals, and carnal cruelty and lust?

24 or am I something greater, which is undiscoverable by mortal senses?"

25 ask yourselves, in the solitudes, and perchance you will not go unanswered! I am the El of Silences!

Chapter 13

1 The words of men are inadequate to express just what man really is, the knowledge of his true nature is beyond the understanding of the unawakened ruach,

2 the inheritance within the grasp of man is without limitation, for it is the totality of all things!

3 man has not been misled in the hope and belief, that the seemingly mortal, is in fact, immortal!

4 the Ruach does not mislead men, they are deceived by their own eyes, they are misled, so they are unable to see things as they are in Reality,

5 all that men see and experience throughout earthly existence is veiled in illusion,

6 man may think his eyes reveal things as they are, but no mortal eye has ever beheld a thing as it actually is, it appears to man through the coloured distorting glass of his own mortality,

7 ruach-ually, men as a whole are little different from the madman who builds himself a kingdom from the fabric of his imagination, yet it was meant to be thus,

8 for man is surrounded by the conditions meet for him, it is for man to discover why this is so, and in discovering, he will find himself! I am The Truth! I am The Reality!

9 this earthly life which I have given you, should not be viewed in its minute aspect, but in the light of Infinitude,

10 all the suffering and disillusionment, the futility, the forlorn hopes and wasted efforts, the oppressions and injustices are not

without a purpose,

11 that purpose is beyond anything man can understand, and infinitely greater than his conception can grasp!

12 the truly awakened man, alone among men, can have any insight into life's end and goal;

13 these are Divine Words, yet they can be set down only in the mere writings of men, and will thus be reduced to things of mortal frailty,

14 mere shapes will be read, and the pattern formed by them will be far short of Truth and Reality,

15 the taste of a fruit or the fragrance of a flower cannot be known by reading about them, the fruit must be eaten, and the flower smelt,

16 only in union with Me, ruach communicating with Ruach, can proof of My Reality be found,

17 yet, because things are as they are, Truth must ever be veiled from man, for who would labour if labourers were paid whether they worked, or not?

18 were they revealed to him, the ignorant man would not comprehend great things, therefore the light is not for him.

Chapter 14

1 The insincere and shallow seeker after diversion and pleasure will find little entertainment in these words,

2 the really earnest man will already know something of the Truth

and will therefore seek it more diligently along a higher path,

3 so these words are given just for those sincere seekers who are aware of their own shortcomings and ignorance, these will be people whose thoughts are not smothered by prejudice, who are not set in their opinions,

4 for who among men is the most confirmed in his opinions? who states things in the most assertive manner and talks with the loudest voice? is it not the most ignorant?

5 I will not let the sincere seeker go unguided, I am The Light on the Path!

6 there are those whose idea of righteousness is mumbled words and repetitious prayers, their souls are warped with selfish desires, and their heaven is the fulfilment of these,

7 their prayers are pleas for pleasure or power, for freedom from the things which develop the ruach,

8 these are the lovers of pleasure and power, which delight in following the path of their own inclinations, they build a creed of their own desires,

9 they have neither courage nor the will to follow a sterner and true path,

10 avoid the companionship of such as these, setting your heart upon the task at hand, rather than the reward, I am The Knower! I am The Rewarder!

11 if a man fixes his attention wholly upon one goal or one thing for his own selfish purpose, as if it were an independent thing, then he moves in darkness of ignorance,

12 if he undertakes a task with a confused mind, not considering the outcome or where it will lead him, or the harm it may do to others or himself, then it is an undertaking of evil,

13 there is a wisdom which knows when to go and when to stay, when to speak and when to remain silent, what is to be done and what is to be left undone,

14 it knows, too, the limitations set by fear and by courage, what constitutes bondage and what freedom,

15 this is the wisdom I have placed at the disposal of man, if he would but seek it! the true wisdom of the Ruach!

16 well do I know the hearts of men, they ever seek to deceive themselves, they clearly see the errors and follies of others, but are blind to their own,

17 the unenlightened men dwelling in comfortable darkness, unperturbed by the challenge of reality as revealed by the light of Truth, lack any understanding of true values,

18 that which appears to them to be no more than a cup of sorrow, is in fact, a chalice filled with the wine of immortality!

19 the vain pleasures that come from pandering to the carnal cravings of the senses appear at first to be a cup of sweetness, but in the end, it is found to hold the brew of bitterness!

Chapter 15

1 He who does right does it not for Me, but for himself, he is the one who benefits, not his Elohim,

2 he who does wrong inflicts himself for it, and he is the sufferer,

3 he who does right does it to his own good, and he who works wickedness does it to his own hurt,

4 it could not be possible, in a just creation, that those whose ways are evil should be dealt with as those who live goodly lives and perform good deeds,

5 the fate of the selfish and that of the unselfish could not be alike! I am the El of Justice, The Maker of the Torah!

6 the ruach of man has the potential for doing all things! it can even rise above earthly limitations, the awakened soul can do whatsoever it wills!

7 man makes the environment for his own development, as it is now, so countless wills from the past have fashioned it, selah;

8 when the body awakens in the morning, it is like a man entering his habitation, it becomes a place of awareness, the soul becomes active in matter; that with which you see, hear, taste, smell, and feel is registered by the soul;

9 physically, the ear of a dead man is still in perfect condition for hearing, but the hearer, the interpreter, has gone; the eyes of a corpse are not blinded, but that which operated them is no longer there;

10 so long as the soul looks outward only, into the deceptive environment of matter, and is satisfied with the material pleasures it finds there, it remains cut off from the greater Realm of the Ruach,

11 it binds itself to matter, failing to find the greater pleasures always there in the silent depths of its soul,

12 confirmed in his attitude by experiences in a deceptive environment, mortal man becomes convinced that all desirable things lie outside himself, he concludes that satisfaction comes from gaining the things which promote material welfare,

13 this is the folly of the unbalanced man,

14 however, balance is the keyword, for it is equally foolish to turn away from material things altogether!

15 man is made of earthly things, because it is intended that he should live and express himself on Earth, it is also intended that he should discover his nature through earthly conditions and experiences,

16 however, when the Divine Spark kindles the ruach, it must not be smothered!

17 balance is the ideal! the soul becoming neither wholly inwardly nor outwardly orientated,

18 man needs his body and must not repudiate it, and if it requires man's labour to sustain it, then is not man entitled to enjoy its pleasures? here also, it is simply a matter of proper balance;

19 man lives in a sea of material manifestation where I am only indirectly reflected, as the soul of man is indirectly reflected in his body,

20 if a man sees with nothing but the eyes of the body, then he cannot perceive Me, for I am beyond his vision, I am the Adon Veiled Behind Matter! I am the Adonai of The Ruach!

21 yet, there is a vision possible to man, which pierces the universal veil! a vision free from all obscurity, a vision uncontaminated by the dark shadows of base desires or fear, by

unstable emotions or unworthy motives,

22 it is the vision seen when man develops a new faculty, a new sense, it is an inward vision of splendour!

23 a wave of Ruach-ual light will engulf him, a mysterious power indescribable in mere words sweeps like a shooting star over the expanse of his ruach, giving a sudden illuminating flash! which floods his whole soul with a glorious light!

24 in its brilliance, he is granted for a brief moment in time, a glimpse of the Vision Splendid, he is then united with the Living Heart of the universe by a bond reaching out to Infinity!

25 nothing known to man, no symbols of his conception, can express the joyousness which floods his whole being,

26 it can be experienced in quiet tranquillity of shalom! it can burst all the bounds of restraint, expressing itself in an all-embracing, overwhelming feeling of love!

27 lost in an unfathomable sea of silent contemplation, the body will shine with radiance from the inner light, and all about will be bathed in a luminous, ruach-ual glow!

28 having once been in Divine communication, these awakened souls know a joy supreme, and never again do they walk through the veil of mortal sorrows,

29 the truly awakened soul is beyond carnal lust and mortal grief, his love is alike for all My creation, and thus he shows supreme love for Me,

30 by this love alone he knows Me in Truth, Who and What I Am, and knowing Me in Truth, he participates in My Whole Being!

31 those who seek union with Me must first prepare a dwelling place for Me in their hearts,

32 but those who are not pure, those who do not fight for Me, those who have not suffered under the discipline of love, and those without wisdom cannot attain union, no matter how much they strive!

33 I am the Elohim of Revelation! I am the Elohim of Enlightenment!

34 would you know the ultimate state of man when he has finally reached his goal? when he has entered into his inheritance of Divinity?

35 it is a state of glory transcending anything conceivable by him during an earthbound existence!

36 his consciousness expands to embrace everything, all that ever was or will be, he sees all, he knows all, he is in all, and he contains all,

37 these things come to him through infinite powers of perception, yet he is above all such powers, he is beyond all yet within all,

38 he is beyond the Realm of Matter, freed from all restrictions, yet he is not denied its joys, and may, if he so desires, manifest again in matter,

39 his thoughts have the power of creation,

40 he is one with the light of lights, the light transcending vision,

41 he is the partaker of My substance, My Son in Eternity! the

inheritor of everlasting life!

42 I am Abba Adonai, Elohim of man.

The Lived Religion - Book 2 - Torot

Chapter 1

1 Everything throughout the whole of creation conforms to certain basic Torot, and where there are Torot, there must be a Torah-maker,

2 there is only one set of unchangeable Torot, so there can be only One Torah-maker,

3 were it otherwise, there would have been a clash of torot, with resultant chaos and confusion, instead of order and stability,

4 the Mishpatim of Elohim are established for the benefit of man!

5 were they not set in stability, man would be nothing but the plaything of chance and the victim of chaos,

6 therefore, on the days of feast and fasting, each following in their due season, I will ever remember the obligations due to my Adon!

7 Torot and Mishpatim are essential to the progress and welfare of mankind,

8 when passions are unrestricted, and weaknesses unfenced by moral torot, various forms of vice and perversions become accepted, and sap the stamina of nations,

9 the Torah of Elohim places an obligation upon mankind to improve itself!

10 every man and woman must safeguard their heritage and raise themselves above earthly sordidness,

11 first, gain complete mastery over the body, and control every urge and desire arising from it! but this is the first step only,

12 the way and means of victory over the flesh are contained in the Torot of the Scriptures, study these diligently,

13 but remember that study and understanding without practice and performance is absolutely futile,

14 first, learn to live as you should! and only then seek to advance further,

15 Torot, though stricken on marble and set up on everlasting pillars, are but diversions for the eye and exercise for the tongue, unless graven also on the tablets of your heart, thus, you shall not fall into error,

16 man directs his life by the Torot of Elohim and the torot of men,

17 the torot of men, which are for the good of men, are to be upheld by the Man of Elohim, who shall not live for the next life alone,

18 a man does not obey Torot because they are the torot of the land, but because they accord with his nature and inclinations,

19 the true nature of man stems from the Adon-ly directive within, and is, therefore, above the edicts of kings.

Chapter 2

1 In upholding the Torot and Mitsvahs of Elohim, the chief concern should be a man's good intent: If he intends well and is

diligent, he can be forgiven much,

2 but if he intends well and is thoughtless, then he shall not be looked upon so kindly;

3 remember, men do not dispense justice, they can but hope to serve it,

4 Elohim alone knows who is good or wicked within his heart, therefore, He alone can dispense true justice!

5 this is the whole Torah needful for man to direct his life: Know your nature, do your duty, and live in harmony with others; to live in harmony means doing wrong to no man,

6 understanding that to do nothing is sometimes wrong, for men are told not to remain passive before the face of evil!

7 there are punishments prescribed for wrongdoing, and much advice given to prevent it,

8 but punishment is only acknowledgement of failure,

9 wrongdoing arises from failure to deal with weaknesses,

10 failure in upbringing, failure in teaching, failure in establishing rules of conduct,

11 and failure in discipline, whether imposed by self or others;

12 when a man comes before the judges for punishment, they do more than half their duty when they condemn him,

13 they should also enquire within themselves, "Wherein have the people failed with this man? was he guided rightly or wrongly? have we no responsibility towards him?"

14 punishing a wrongdoer without seeking out the cause of his deeds is hypocritical justice!

15 if a man who walks in the darkness stumbles into a pit, is he to blame? if the light bearers be too feeble to keep men from stumbling, their light is of no value,

16 therefore, if a brother fall into a pit by the wayside, the bearers of light cannot be guiltless;

17 a nation was once made from the blood of kings, and it became great and good; the Torah of Truth was revealed to this nation and it rejoiced in the light,

18 but, in a few generations it accepted the light as being something to which it was entitled by heritage, so the nation became careless in the preservation of the light,

19 the winds of adversity came, and the light was blown out.

Chapter 3

1 As the smell of putrefaction assails the nostrils of men, so does wickedness give forth something which assails those in the other realm, wickedness is therefore an offence against them,

2 if a man threw filth over the wall into your courtyard, would you not consider this an act of hostility?

3 could any among you live in harmony with those who were insensitive to your own sensitivity?

4 the Almighty El neither rewards nor punishes, for He has established the Torah whereby each man decrees his own fate,

5 therefore, give due respect to the Torah of Elohim! walk in His Ways and bow to His Decrees! you are placed on Earth that His Purpose may be fulfilled,

6 therefore fight not against His Will, nor rebel against His Torot, lest you bring about your own destruction!

7 the Almighty El will not destroy the transgressor, for that man will destroy himself!

8 each man ultimately decrees his own fate and receives his reward or punishment, according to the Torah, selah;

9 My Design is unrevealed to the multitude, few are the men who can understand why I planted the road to the Place of Glory with sharp stones of suffering and pain, or why life is a struggle through the thorny forest of adversity,

10 I am the Creator! in Whose Ruach-image and likeness you were fashioned, and My Torot ordained your present estate and circumstances upon Earth,

11 in My sight all men are equal, and I judge them as men and not according to their estate,

12 the rich and the poor, the highborn and the lowly, the wise and the simple all receive a fitting reward according to their labours,

13 from each is expected results according to his abilities, from some much and from others little;

14 know that only that which serves the Purpose of the Great Adonai is accounted worthy by Me,

15 obey My Mitsvahs, take heed of the Mishpatim I have made,

for they conform to your needs,

16 all things are bent to the benefit of man,

17 and all that encompasses your life accord with My Direction,

18 that the soul within you may enjoy continued gracious growth from stage to stage of life's unfolding!

19 so that when the cumbersome sheath of mortal flesh is cast off, your soul may receive a just and fitting compensation under My Great Torah, in accordance with its thoughts and deeds on Earth!

20 brothers, now that you are invested with new life, open your eyes! and behold the works of The Supreme Elohim with understanding!

21 always follow the path you have been shown, so that your steps lead you towards perfection,

22 never incline towards degrading thoughts or look into the eyes of lust, for these things have led great men astray and brought down mighty ones,

23 be clean in all ways, be clean within and without, in body, thought, word, and deed,

24 work for the Adonai Most High, and He will work for you, He remembers well the man who labours on His behalf,

25 he who labours to the benefit of others works for the Great Adonai, he who improves Earth, works for Him!

26 the true temples of the Great Adonai are not structures of stone and brick, they are places of quietude in your heart and home where you listen to the awakening of your soul, as it responds to

conscious contact with Him,

27 His worship is your labour among the people,

28 His praise is the song in your heart,

29 His adoration is your joy of living!

Chapter 4

1 Keep the shalom of Adonai and maintain the order of His Torah among men and women, for they are His flocks and herds, and He calls forth shepherds from among them,

2 He made Earth a workplace for man and not a pleasure garden, therefore, be you a songleader at the task,

3 He is the Mighty El! The Nameless One Whom your fathers held in awe!

4 He it was Who dissipated the darkness over the waters, Who separated the chaos, Who lifted the cloud, Who made the breezes of life to fill the nostrils of men!

5 the ways of a man are always right in his own eyes, but they deceive him, and unless he has guidance of the Torah, he is led astray,

6 but where is the Torah today? is it where it should be, inscribed on the living hearts of the people? or is it a thing written on dead scrolls? rolled up and discarded?

7 we make of our lives what we will,

8 destiny supplies us with the yarn which we weave into a pattern

of beauty and utility, or tangle up into a hopeless wasteful confusion, where are the craftsman spinners today?

9 if you are ignorant of the Torah, complain not of that about which you have no knowledge, seek rather to understand its nature, and thus know the meaning of life!

10 he who understands the Torah knows why the pattern of life is as it is, why it is a design of light and shade,

11 the Torah is unchangeable and unchallengeable, and none but a fool rants against that which cannot be altered,

12 man will never find contentment until he learns to accept the Torah as it has been established, it governs the whole Earth and his life, to live in harmony with it is to live in shalom!

13 if, in your weakness and waywardness, you find the burden of the Torah intolerable, all your lamentations and wailing will not ease the load, it will do nothing but add to your distress,

14 the Torah concedes nothing to the weaknesses of men!

15 riches cannot buy life, nor can gold purchase back wasted hours, therefore, employ the future that you have left to your greatest benefit,

16 lament not that you were born or desire that life should depart, life has a purpose and meaning, even for one as miserable as you, and your obligations may not be set aside;

17 men will argue about the distinctions of words, but they would be better engaged in studying the Torah in its entirety,

18 it is immutable, it decrees the circumstances which surround your sojourn on Earth,

19 yet, it has established that by the nature of things, for all reasonable desires, all honest endeavours, and for all normal requirements, there is attainment and success!

20 the present alone is yours, and future fortunes will be dispensed by the Will of the Great Adonai in accordance with His Design,

21 therefore, you cannot know what the unborn days will bring forth,

22 as to your own soul and your future state, subject to the Torah, it is being conceived in your present thoughts and deeds.

The Lived Religion - Book 3 - Soul

Chapter 1

1 Today, men seek to gather where they have not planted, they desire the increase, but disdain the effort,

2 they seek to benefit through the toil of others, unproductive tongues move vigorously, while skilled hands are idle,

3 men must learn that no more can be taken from the storehouse than was placed in there;

4 where are the men of self-assurance? the men of straight tongue and of constant speech? that were known of yore?

5 today, if an ass were king men would bray,

6 this is the day when fine speech flourishes, but it lacks substance, it falls from the tongue and is lost on the wind,

7 the words of the night are soaked in honey, but as day dawns, they melt away with the dews of morning,

8 even the words of lovers are sweet for but a time, tomorrow they turn to bitterness and gall,

9 O for the days that were, the joyous days now past, when words were things of substance with but one meaning!

10 now, my days are without object, they are spent in stringing and unstringing my lyre, while the song I wish to sing remains mute in my heart,

11 I do not look for the overthrow of evil, I do not bewail the

existence of wickedness, these will always be while man remains mortal,

12 wickedness will flourish even in the House of Elohim, for has He not ordained in the Torah to permit a poisonous weed to grow among healing herbs?

13 neither do I seek for any undue reward, nor do I consider my goodness deserves it, yet, I would enjoy some pleasure undiluted with sorrow,

14 for now, even at the bottom of the rare cup of joy, lies the dregs of bitterness and sorrow;

15 because my tongue did not turn around corners and twist back on itself, because the words I spoke came from my heart,

16 undiluted with any malicious thought,

17 because I chided the rich for their selfishness and inconsideration, their wasteful living and meaningless activities, they became my enemies,

18 because I called upon the powerful to live according to the Torot they professed to uphold, and the Words declared to be Kodesh, I was seized and imprisoned,

19 when I protested the injustice to the ears of the people, I was beaten with rods, I was branded as "One who seeks to destroy the stability of the land,"

20 I, who tried to set an example of goodness, to lead a life dedicated to my Elohim, to convert the wicked to righteousness, am myself declared wicked by the workers of evil!

21 why is this, O my Adon? have I, to my sorrow and undoing,

weighed the values of Your Torah wrongly?

22 I, who was once a man of estate, am now poor, I have been deprived of all I possess,

23 I supported the oppressed against the powerful and lent my arm to the lowly,

24 I threw my own riches into the balances, to counter the injustices of the rich,

25 and what has been my reward from those to whom I gave aid and succour? do they not mock me and hold me in contempt?

26 am I not called a fool even by them?

27 I am thrown crusts of bread in pity, but no man calls me friend,

28 I speak to men, but they become restless and remember things which call them away,

29 the sight of me causes men to quicken their steps and change the direction of their journey,

30 has goodness, then, become a plague in the land?

31 I have sought but to turn others from wickedness, and to replace their misdeeds with deeds of goodness!

32 I have sought to revalue virtue! so that it becomes honoured among men, not merely a plaything of words, but a treasure held in the heart,

33 yet, men mock me, they say, "These are things in which we too believe, but no man can wholly live by them,

34 they are not the substance of life, and none but a fool discards the substance for the shadow!"

35 where is my dwelling? is it not occupied by one who wrings tears from widows and steals the food of orphans?

36 the wicked one sleeps on a bed of comfort, the righteous one lays his head upon a stone;

37 the wicked one contemplates his end with contentment, a fine burial and earthly honour awaits him,

38 the righteous one will mingle his bones with those of dogs and cattle;

39 where are my servants? do they not toil for one who deals with them harshly? who rejoices at the sweat that pours down on their labours?

40 the wicked one sits on the seats of comfort, he wallows in an over-abundance of good things,

41 while the righteous one squats in the burning sun, he is grateful for a few crumbs and a little water;

42 the wicked one never lacks the delights and services of women, the righteous one lacks even a smile of compassion, a hand to touch his head;

43 where are my children, the comfort and consolation of an old man? do they not labour with bitterness of heart?

44 bearing the scorn poured upon the grey head of their father with unrewarding fortitude?

45 the wicked ones display their riches and mock my children,

46 saying, "All this is ours to enjoy, or give others at our pleasure! where then is your reward?"

47 the righteous one cannot give even a piece of rag to patch the garments of his offspring, or a morsel of food to ease their hunger;

48 where are my riches? where my estate? are they not enjoyed by the avaricious and haughty? the sly man and the cunning man? the hypocrite and deceiver?

49 the wicked ones have no thought of righteousness and virtue, they are clad in comfort and filled to fullness,

50 while the righteous one has half a garment, and his next meal is unseen;

51 O Supreme Elohim! is Earth the heritage of the wicked? or the heritage of the good?

52 if goodness is to be won for Earth by example, then what must I do?

53 if by words, what more can I say? if by weapons, can an unarmed man fight a multitude?

54 where have I failed? I do not know, I have no answer, I believe, I hope,

55 I am an old man bowed down with the cares of an old man, the fires of youth are burned out, leaving just the grey comfortless ashes,

56 when men ask, I answer, "I do not know," can any man answer more truthfully?

57 hear this! this man's success was in his failure, in trying to change others, he changed himself!

58 each effort was a shaping stroke to glory!

59 Earth is as it should be, it cannot be changed, but if a man would change himself to his own benefit, he must ever strive and seek to change the Earth,

60 the message of this writing is not one of futility, but one of hope, no man could have better shaped his future.

Chapter 2

1 Awful is the Great Day of Judgment at its dawning in the Netherworld!

2 the soul stands naked in the Hall of Judgment, nothing can now be hidden, hypocrisy is no avail,

3 to maintain goodness when the soul reveals its own repulsiveness is futile,

4 to mumble empty ritual is foolishness,

5 to call upon elohim who have no existence is a waste of time,

6 behold, in the Great Hall every man is judged! on that Day and henceforth, his qualities shall form his food,

7 his soul, soft as clay upon Earth, is hardened and set into shape at death, according to its moulding during life!

8 the balances are adjusted; Truth is the assessor; one arrives:

9 Shall he dwell among beauty as an elohim-ling? or be given captive to the Keeper of Horrors, to dwell among vile things under a merciful mantle of darkness?

10 one arrives: The twisted body and the ugly face have gone, discarded at the portal,

11 he strides through the Hall in radiance! to pass into the Place of Everlasting Beauty!

12 one arrives: Now no earthly body shields the horror which is the true likeness of the evildoer upon Earth,

13 he runs from the light, which he cannot tolerate, and hides himself in the shadows near the Place of Terror,

14 soon he will be drawn to his compatible place among Dismal Company!

15 one arrives: He has been upright and a just one, his failings and weaknesses were of little account,

16 this upright man fears nothing, for he is welcomed among the Bright Ones, and shall go unhampered among the Everlasting Adonai!

17 one arrives: He trembles before the Unseen Judge, he is lost, he knows nothing, earthly knowledge and confidence are left behind,

18 the balance drops, he sees his soul and recognises his true self, he rushes into the merciful darkness,

19 it enfolds him, and dark arms embrace him, drawing him into the terrible gloom, into the Place of Dark Secret Horrors!

20 one arrives: She graced the court with beauty where men sang of her loveliness and grace, now, as when a mantle is removed, all is discarded, it is the Time of Unveiling!

21 who can describe the lustful thoughts and secret unclean deeds which fashioned the horror coming through the portal? there is a hush among the compassionate!

22 one arrives: On Earth she was pitied by the compassionate and scorned by the hard-hearted,

23 there, her lot was degradation and servitude, privation and sacrifice, few and meagre were the gifts from life, yet she triumphed!

24 now, she comes forward surrounded by brilliance, even the Shining Ones are dazzled by her beauty!

25 one arrives: The twisted face and pain-wracked body of the cripple have been left behind, a kind and loving soul dwelt imprisoned within its confines,

26 now, the relieved ruach steps forward into the Great Hall, unencumbered and free, glorious to behold!

27 one arrives: The splendid body which graced Earth remains there, an empty, decaying thing,

28 the naked soul enters the Everlasting Halls, it is a deformed, misshapen thing fit only to dwell in the merciful gloom of the place with which it has compatible affinity!

29 read, O children of the unborn years, and absorb the wisdom of the past, which is your heritage,

30 the enlightening words from a past, which is to you in days so far away, and yet in truth, so near!

Chapter 3

1 The Earth is not for the pleasure of man, but it is a place of instruction for his soul,

2 does a man not more readily feel the stirrings of his ruach in the face of disaster, than in the lap of luxury?

3 the tuition of the soul is a long and arduous course, of instruction, discipline, and training!

4 Heaven: Where perfection visualised on Earth may be realised, and desires and ideals materialised, where hard-striven-for aspirations are attained,

5 it is the place where all the properly developed ruach-ual potential latent in man reaches maturity and fulfilment!

6 Earth: The place of training, development, and preparation, the testing ground,

7 the battlefield, where men discover their true natures when confronted by life's challenges, contests, and contentions,

8 where competition and controversy are the rule,

9 it is here that aims and objectives are conceived and thought out for realisation later in the proper place,

10 it is a starting point, the beginning of the journey, it is here that the proper road must be wisely chosen!

11 when death calls for you, let him not find you ill-equipped and unprepared,

12 in the final hour, which must surely come, there will be no opportunity for fine speech and nought can delay his command,

13 then all the possessions you have cherished and stored will be as nought, and all you will be able to take with you will be that which you have fashioned within;

14 do not be numbered among the foolish, who say, "Time enough, for I am yet young,"

15 death claims the breast-child as well as the aged, and on this you should ponder,

16 consider well your future estate!

17 here, you are the architect of your future abode,

18 Earth is the place of sowing, Heaven is the place of reaping,

19 here, you are the sculptor who chisels the statue, the potter who fashions the pot, the woodworker who carves the pillar,

20 what is there on Earth more deserving of your care and attention, than your own future form, appearance, and destination?

Chapter 4

1 You ask for words to guide, and I answer thus:

2 Be still, be quiet, shabbat in silence with tranquillity of heart,

3 calm the restless surges of unbidden thoughts, the oppressions of uncontrolled desires,

4 there, in the stillness and silence, you will be a shining, motionless, unflickering light, like a flame of a candle on a windless night,

5 that is the pure flame of self! the light that guides towards Divinity,

6 it is the small light of Eternal wisdom, lit from the Infinite Flame of Truth;

7 the path of shalom is not always the path of progress,

8 the path of pleasure is pleasant, while the path of progress is beset with pain and strife,

9 but let your ruach be at shalom, for things happen as they will, it is the grain being winnowed from the chaff;

10 only the good vessel is worthy of the fire, it is burnt, that its shape may be set and its design endure,

11 so be aware, it is always easier for men to follow the ways of the flesh than the ways of the Ruach,

12 there is a ladder which rises before you:

13 Its two supports are experience in the body and experience in the ruach, the rungs are your daily deeds, and your thoughts and fantasies of your earthly life,

14 now is the test, will your daily deeds and secret thoughts support your ascent? or, are they incapable of bearing you upward?

Chapter 5

1 We are taught that we live forever, and this is true, selah; but it is equally true that no moment of life must be wasted,

2 for each hour and day on Earth is a shaping for the future!

3 we are the inheritors of a portion of time, we can dissipate it on futile things, or utilise it to our everlasting benefit,

4 the span of man's life is neither long nor short, but sufficient for its purpose,

5 whatever benefits a man wishes to attain for his soul may be attained in his lifetime,

6 a lifetime is sufficient to fashion the soul to ultimate glory or to ultimate horror!

7 what end would a longer life serve? to the wicked, an opportunity for more evil,

8 to the selfish, more time to hurt others, and to the miserly more time to lay up worthless things,

9 the slothful ones would rejoice, for there would be more time for their idleness!

10 each man's life should leave its impress on Earth, and each man should depart a better man for having lived!

11 every sorrowful blow that falls upon the soul is a tempering stroke, the metal that suffers the fires of the furnace longest is the finest in quality,

12 sorrow, suffering, and the afflictions which beset men are not sent wilfully,

13 they are necessities for existence, without which the slumbering soul could not awaken, they are needful for its development,

14 therefore is it not a vain hope and foolishness to expect miracles to protect you? and prevent you from deriving the benefit of these experiences?

15 is it reasonable to expect exemption from the things you were born to experience?

16 therefore, accept with good grace that which life bestows on you,

17 is it not better to endure manfully the things which are unavoidable?

18 the scales are never wholly unbalanced: A loss is recorded to adversity, and a gain is recorded to experience,

19 joy is taken from the body, and strength is added to the soul,

20 but even enter the habitation of joy with caution, for a heady brew is served therein, which can call forth the demons of mischief and madness!

21 the Torah is fixed, unchangeable, not so your soul, for here you alone are responsible for its appearance,

22 remember that every thought and deed is a thread in the pattern of the fabric, so think well, will the tapestry be a thing of beauty? or of ugliness?

23 the soul can be whatever it wills itself to be, it is the fashioner of its own form and destiny.

Chapter 6

1 As the great sycamore resides in a tiny seed, so does your soul occupy your body,

2 and as the dark soil wherein the seed is planted to the sunlit splendour above, so is this life to the life beyond the tomb!

3 as health is to the body, so is conscience to the soul,

4 that man is a soul residing within a body is the most obvious of truths, though seek not to understand it too perfectly,

5 for understanding is a quality of the soul itself, and this has to be awakened;

6 your soul came into the body as a new turn of the scroll, the sheet is clean, ready for use, but what you write thereon is recorded forever!

7 your soul is as a newly cut block of marble, upon which every thought and deed strikes a blow,

8 it is as fresh clay cast upon the potter's wheel, you alone are the craftsman for the fashioning of your soul, you alone are the artist of the design,

9 is it a bright thing of joyous beauty formed by goodness? or is it a dark corrupt horror deformed by vice and wickedness?

10 ask these things of your ruach, for only it knows what lies

hidden within;

11 to nourish and groom the body is by no means undesirable, but take care that you neglect not the soul,

12 the body comes, it grows and decays, the soul remains forever, therefore cherish the everlasting soul, for it is your own true self,

13 glorify your body! cherish it, keep it well, for it is the dwelling place of the soul,

14 and is not such a master worthy of a well kept habitation?

15 to revile or mortify the body is a wickedness, for thus, you desecrate the most glorious temple on Earth!

16 as ground must be prepared for the barley, and clay kneaded for the wheel, so has your body to be prepared for the fulfilling of its purpose,

17 therefore let the soul rule your body unchallenged! for if there be revolt, then you are torn asunder;

18 health is the reflection of harmony between soul and body,

19 with what do you smell? with your nose? is not the nose intact on a corpse?

20 and the eye? does it see when the ruach departs?

21 like an oar without an oarsman, like a sail without a wind, like a bow without a bowman, like a dwelling without an inhabitant, such is the body without the soul;

22 my ruach departs to its abode, beyond the power of sharp sword, beyond the reach of thrusting spear, beyond the range of

swift arrow,

23 face to face with what must be and cannot be altered, face to face with the ultimatum of destiny, cease from sorrow.

Chapter 7

1 What is this passing thing called life? this fragile flower so tenderly cherished, seen in its true frailty, here on the field of blood? does it have any real meaning?

2 here on the field of blood the dead sleep to awake to glory!

3 but to the victorious ones remaining alive there is glory on Earth, so, do not dally here with the dying,

4 arise, go to your proper reward and lay me down to mine; fear not for me, already I see the welcoming light beyond the veil! we shall meet again!

5 now, the years of earthly instruction are left behind,

6 the last lesson is read, the pupil has departed to take up his appointed task,

7 he has been born to life! and death has been left behind! there are no dead, just the departed living,

8 death alone occupies the tomb; death is a selah at the beginning of life, a hesitation before the light of a greater day!

9 death is a deceiver, a non-existent thing of the shadows,

10 from the creeping caterpillar comes the light-loving butterfly, and from the hard grain, the full blooming barley,

11 who, looking at the date stone, can see therein the tree to be? search the seed, and the plant is nowhere to be found, even so, is it with man and his ruach,

12 to live, man must believe in his soul,

13 and this belief comes not from outside teaching, but from listening to its whispers, unbelief comes from stopping the ears to its murmurs,

14 read the Kodesh Writings diligently, and hear the voice of the Instructing Ruach with receptive heart!

15 so you may furnish your soul with nourishment, and it shall not wither from any lack of sustenance!

16 the future destiny and circumstances of the soul are shaped in the earthly body,

17 when in the hour of its release the soul takes flight, freed from its earthly container of flesh, it assumes the form moulded by its desires,

18 in that awesome Day of Reckoning, the wicked shall be revealed in hideous shape, but the upright shall step forward in splendour!

19 neither life nor love ends at the Grim Portal, the strength of the invisible bond between two souls binds them even after death,

20 that which binds strongest of all is love, love which is sincere, true, and constant! such love endures through tribulations and trials,

21 if one you love has departed through the gates into the Great

Halls of Eternity, then be comforted by these words of Truth:

22 The Guardian at the Grim Portal is no fearsome being,

23 but a compassionate attendant, who tends you gently while asleep, until the morning of a more glorious day!

24 then, you will be awakened to journey through a greater adventure with the companions of former times,

25 but, if your companion did not cherish their soul on earth, your meeting will be one of lament!

Chapter 8

1 What became of the loveliness which once clothed you on Earth? whose fault that you brought it not with you?

2 did you ever pause, even for one moment, to gaze into the self-revealing mirror within? and see the awful creature you were forming?

3 amid pleasures and luxury, did you not think of the wellbeing of your inner self? did you not care?

4 O, if I could help you now, but the hideousness was set firm in the furnace-fire of death,

5 then, the enveloping flesh was stripped away and the hidden horror within the mould revealed;

6 as the butterfly emerges from the chrysalis, so should the soul emerge from its earthly body,

7 but an unnatural thing like this was never intended, yet you

freely made the choice, not a single disfiguring line was made by another;

8 yes, I loved you on Earth, nothing there was more precious to me than my love,

9 I forgave her wilfulness and was not stirred up when her words were unkind,

10 I ever remained a man of cool temper,

11 I clothed her well, and good food she never lacked,

12 my heart sang in her presence! I rejoiced in her loveliness,

13 she was my life, my wife! yet, she was unfaithful,

14 she was cruel, she found pleasure in deceit and perversion,

15 O horror, O terror, O cringing fear, keep away from me!

16 O my eyes, O my heart, it is true, it is the one I loved!

17 O let me die once more, that consciousness may pass from me! it is her whom I loved,

18 she for whom I waited in joyful anticipation, hoping to find the light of my youth,

19 hoping the overlay of later evils would be sloughed away by death, hoping to find the warm, throbbing liveliness I once held!

20 I would gladly have forgiven the pain she caused me on Earth!

21 O what has become of the smooth flesh? the warm touch? where is the beauty of face? the grace of form?

22 raise not the crocodile-skinned arms to shield the awful snout! I cannot bear to behold the green-rimmed, red-veined eyes!

23 O racing heart! I hear misformed words amidst the hiss and gurgle issuing forth from the oozing aperture! O sorrow!

24 say not that I was so blind, so greatly deceived, that you cared for nought but the earthly things we shared,

25 that your affection was the false front of hypocrisy, your love a lie,

26 with whom did you share the terrible thoughts and desires that fashioned you thus? surely, this cannot be the work of your own nature alone;

27 did I not always forgive? was I not always patient?

28 fickle you were, and pleasure loving, selfish, cruel, and deceitful, but all this I forgave because of the plea of my heart, was this not enough?

29 O, where is the companion I awaited? lost, and worse than lost!

30 O compassion, O mercy, come to my aid! my heart fails me, I cannot face what I thought to greet so joyously,

31 O powers of solicitude, strengthen me!

32 what can I do to mitigate the Torah? is there hope? is there a way?

33 a whisper of comfort, selah; O, gratefully I hear it:

34 "Between this self-shaped horror and the Glorious Ones, there is an uncrossable chasm, in sorrow and anguish, it must seek a road, it must go its own dark way, as you must go yours in the light,

35 turn back, turn again towards the light! the compassion in your own heart does nought to bridge the gulf between, unless it strikes a responsive spark within the other heart;

36 the trials and sorrows borne so well, the uncomplaining unselfishness fashioned you in glory,

37 nor would you have reached the present degree of perfection, had she not been as she was and is now revealed to be,

38 this fearful fate was wrought by the lost one alone, for each is the sole keeper of his ruach,

39 each soul is fashioned by every thought, desire, and deed, every emotion that touched it during its sojourn in an earthly body,

40 each is the maker of his own future, the fashioner of his own being!

41 let the memory be erased, this is no longer the companion of your path."

Chapter 9

1 The first duty of man is to know himself and to reflect upon his destiny, to become aware of his soul, and this he cannot do in the house of pleasure, in the arms of joy,

2 therefore, is sorrow not apportioned to man in wisdom and

consideration?

3 though one should also avoid the dwelling place of sorrow, for there, good is transmuted into evil, and wails of self-pity sadden the heavy night,

4 the tear-damp mist which issues from within withers the flowers which bedeck the garden of life;

5 better to stray not into either dwelling, but walk the path of moderation between them;

6 no other elohim knows how to call Him by Name,

7 even the greatest of them being less than a servant before Him,

8 yet this I have been told, that the ruach of man can know this Great Adonai and can even know His nature,

9 therefore, perchance the ruach of man is greater than any of the elohim!

10 but who am I to presume to call upon the Most High Adonai of All? I, who am not without wickedness and weak in ruach,

11 I have filled my heart with knowledge of the Kodesh Writings, but still I fear the judgment,

12 I am not weak in my standing with earthly things, but I am weak beside You,

13 will I, too, ever be worthy of the grandeur of the Eternal Mansions?

14 man can swim against the current towards the bank, but he needs a helping hand to pull him ashore when he is exhausted

from the struggle,

15 O Great Being Whose nature is beyond understanding, grant me just a spark of the Eternal wisdom, that it might light my soul and kindle the flame of immortal life!

16 what is the destined fate of a man who knows the existence of things beyond his understanding? I see, but I do not know, therefore I am afraid,

17 a man may believe he knows his destiny, but he cannot be assured with certainty, in no other way can he fulfil it,

18 in this way alone can his soul be properly awakened to flower with its full potential;

19 this is the fate of man: He must strive for that which he cannot attain,

20 he must believe in that which he cannot prove,

21 he must seek that which he cannot find,

22 he must travel a road without knowing his destination, only thus can the purpose of life be fulfilled;

23 knowing this should strengthen man during his sojourn on Earth:

24 The purpose of all human life is a goal so glorious it surpasses all earthly understanding!

25 we may visualise our individual Heaven as we will, it is ordained that we have this freedom,

26 how close or how far we are from Reality is of little

consequence, what is, is;

27 he who seeks a non-existent destination, will, nevertheless, get somewhere,

28 while he who seeks not at all will get nowhere.

Chapter 10

1 Earthly life fulfils itself without attainment! selah;

2 of all desirable things attainable by man, the assurance of his immortality, clear insight into the purpose behind his creation, and true knowledge of the road towards the fulfilment of his destiny are the greatest,

3 those are the most desirable things on Earth, and so they are the most highly priced and difficult to attain!

4 consider from whence man came:

5 His place of origin is like the clay pit, where men toil to dig the raw materials used by the potter,

6 a piece of clay is dug out and separated,

7 it comes from the darkness of the pit into the light of day, even so is a man born,

8 the clay is cast on the wheel to be turned, the wheel spins, and the soft clay is moulded into shape,

9 if the shape be good and pleasing to the eye it will be kept and cherished,

10 if it be ill-shaped, it is cast aside, discarded and unwanted, a useless thing;

11 the potter is man, the clay his soul, and the wheel is life;

12 swift and fleet of foot is the brief life of mortal man,

13 though it be numbered in days and counted in years, yet he lives from moment to moment,

14 and knows not whether he has a few or many days left to squander or utilise, can it all be futile? all in vain?

15 can life, when it passes, be as though it never were?

16 are the days of man no more than wind whispers among the trees? or fish trails through the waters?

17 the days of men are as a strong breeze sweeping a boat swiftly towards harbour, the journey is soon over, the voyage is quickly ended,

18 he arrives at his destination weak and weary, heavy-limbed and toil-worn,

19 the sun is setting, night hastens on with quiet footfalls, the darkness gathers in the remains of day, and the home-sick wanderer finds shalom!

20 without the dwelling the heavy darkness of night gathers, the rustle of life is stilled,

21 the mantle of blackness closes around the weary-footed wayfarer who is nearing the end of the journey to his everlasting abode, selah;

22 he arrives and enters through the welcoming portals with a great sigh of relief, selah,

23 he casts aside his dust-stained garments and sinks down into the soft couch of forgetfulness,

24 the wanderer is home! the tired hoary head has found its place of shalom!

25 behold, like a falcon soaring up into the sunlight, man, for a brief span in the immensity of time, is borne upward on wings of life!

26 then, the high flight is over,

27 he descends,

28 the wings are folded,

29 and he seeks the solitude of his silent resting place.

Chapter 11

1 There is an end to all earthly things! and all men must come at last to the appointed place,

2 none has gold or treasure enough to buy even one more day of time, there is no way back, it is the place of no return,

3 here the prince and the bondsman are alike, here they stand side by side, and none can tell who was the man of high rank and who the lowly one,

4 that which distinguishes them now is something not of Earth, though that is where it was acquired;

5 as the waters drain away from the land into the channels and from the channels into the river, to be borne away and lost in the great green sea,

6 so does man sink down into oblivion, never to return as himself, he is gone from Earth forever,

7 back to the place from whence he sprang, back to his Eternal home, selah;

8 now, the sleepers sleep not, for The Time has arrived!

9 their slumber was not counted as men count days and hours, they awakened even as one awakes from a sleep,

10 awake now in the Day of Destiny! some to inherit a future of radiant glory, and some disgraceful shame and shapelessness!

11 what kind of stars encircle the vault lying above?

12 what companion lightens the burden of the never-ending night?

13 what whisper breaks through the dark solitude?

14 how many sleepers lie enwrapped in the dusty silence? whose voice will awaken them? and on what distant Day?

15 with what greetings will they be called forth?

16 those things, I, myself, cannot know, yet I search the Old Scripts and am reassured, for they who wrote, did so from some certain knowledge,

17 there were things known to them which are lost to our days,

18 therefore, let it now be written, and as written, let it be made known: The One Elohim is above all in greatness!

19 but under Him, above all else on Earth, is the soul of man!

Chapter 12

1 The soul of man is not isolated from Elohim above, nor from the mortal body below, for it is that which spans the gulf between,

2 it is the link between Elohim and man, between immortal and mortal!

3 nothing exists, which is or can be isolated from all else,

4 there is a connection between Earth and the Region of Glory, a link between dust and star,

5 from the Highest Adonai down to the mote runs an unbroken and unbreakable chain,

6 yet, man is apart from all other creatures, in that he has foreknowledge of death and decay,

7 if man be immortal, then it is the burden of his immortality,

8 but if he passes to nothingness, he is cursed above the unknowing beasts, which know not the dread of approaching doom!

9 something unseen animates the inert clay of your being, something intangible is added to the earthly material of your body,

10 think not primarily of your material self, for within your body resides the soul, which activates the thinking heart,

11 and is not the resident of the dwelling of greater importance than the materials of its construction?

12 gaze upon a corpse and see, it is empty of life, something that was is no longer there, the soul is missing,

13 the soul delights in sweet smells and knows the perfumes of Earth by the performance of the nose,

14 it rejoices in delicacies of the table and tastes them only through the workings of the mouth,

15 food feeds the flesh, but the flesh finds no pleasure in eating,

16 for it is the soul which experiences the enjoyment of food,

17 the eyes are the sentinels which keep watch for you, the lights that go before your path, as braziers before a caravan,

18 yet, they see not of themselves, for they are but the instruments of sight, without a consciousness of their own,

19 it is the soul within which interprets their messages;

20 that man has a soul is beyond all doubt, it is the most obvious of all truths, seek not to delve unduly into its secrets, but harmonise it with your body,

21 commune with your soul, and awaken its potentialities!

22 intellect, reason, willpower, and comprehension, these are not the soul,

23 they are the manifestations of its existence, its attributes and its activity, but they are not the soul itself,

24 stimulate the soul by contact with that to which it responds, know it through its manifestations, and understand it through its faculties.

Chapter 13

1 The soul is yours to fashion, it can be made radiant by goodness, beautified by virtue, and glorified by love,

2 it can be hideously deformed by vices and passions, and twisted into a form of distorted horror by meanness and hatred,

3 it cannot be valued too greatly! nor can it be handled too carefully, for it is your own true self, the reality which is you,

4 it is as virgin stone for you to cut and shape as you will, but remember, the image carved is not easily altered,

5 and shall one day be displayed to the Eyes of Eternity in its true likeness! though on Earth, this is now veiled by the flesh,

6 the soul is bodiless within the body, everlasting among things that change and pass away!

7 man does not perceive his soul, because his senses face outward from the soul, towards earthly things with which it makes contact,

8 so it is that only the most developed of men can close out the material things about them, and turn their senses inward to perceive the soul;

9 the soul looks out through the eyes and sees all which is

without, but nothing of this can look in through the eyes and see the soul,

10 even though the soul's feeling may be reflected there; an eye without a soul behind it sees nothing;

11 that by which we know the texture of things, by which we taste, smell and hear,

12 by which we experience the tenderness and suffering of love, and perceive the beauty of nature,

13 by which we value the glory of self sacrifice,

14 by that we are also assured of something immortal within us,

15 for when a man comes to the realisation that it is by the soul within him that he knows and experiences all things about him, he has taken the first great step towards conscious immortality!

16 when the body and soul are torn apart, what remains?

17 no man lives by the air he breathes, it is something more, the soul, that gives life.

Chapter 14

1 Naked does man come from his mother's womb, and naked does he return to the womb of the Earth,

2 he brings no possessions with him to Earth, and no more can be taken out, yet, he leaves not altogether as he entered,

3 for though his riches and estate, his titles, even his clothes are left behind, if he has lived wisely, he goes out richer in soul-

wisdom and arrayed in soul-beauty,

4 man arrives at the Great Portal arrayed in glory! or clothed in horror!

5 rejoice in the sure knowledge of your soul's indestructibility,

6 but let your joy be leavened by remembrance of your responsibility for its condition,

7 in the newborn childling is the soft seed of the slumbering soul, this will be developed, moulded, and fashioned throughout the period of its earthly existence,

8 it will be shaped by man himself to his own inner likeness,

9 then, when stripped of its outward bodily covering, man will stand revealed to himself and be faced with splendour or horror,

10 in the likeness to which the soul is fashioned in the body, so shall it come forth in the ruach on its appointed Day!

11 the body is a womb, life the days of conception, and death the birth of the soul,

12 is it not written, "Some shall bring forth monsters and fearful things? and some shall bear elohim?" these things are not beyond understanding;

13 once, a prophet taught the people that every man is his own mother, and they fed him to the crocodiles,

14 children cannot be told even half the truth, but must be led by childish tales towards understanding.

Chapter 15

1 The Song of the Soul. I am the sleeper awakened from slumber,

2 I am the seed of life Eternal,

3 I am the everlasting hope of man,

4 I am a shoot of the Ruach Divine, I am the soul, I have been since the beginning of time and shall be forever,

5 I am the design interwoven in the warp and weft of creation,

6 I am the indestructible essence of life,

7 I am the treasure chest of man's hopes and aspirations, the storehouse of lost loves and fulfilled dreams;

8 before time, I was an unconscious ruach potential, united with the Supreme,

9 ever since time began, I was in the slumbering sea of ruchot, waiting to be drawn forth into mortal incarnation;

10 though the mortal body enwrapping me fall apart and decay, I remain everlasting and immortal,

11 through all the ebb and flow of life, whatever destiny decrees, I remain the everlasting jewel of ages, invisible to mortal eyes and untouchable by mortal hands,

12 I am the Eternal part of mortal man, ever awaiting the awakening kiss, the whisper of recognition,

13 O being of flesh, deny me not! let me not dwell in forgotten solitude, left alone, unwanted and unheeded,

14 hold me to you as a lover holds their beloved, reach out beyond earthly things and kiss the lips that are yours eternally,

15 look out beyond the realm of earthly opposites, out beyond the pettiness of gains and possessions,

16 grasp and possess me, your own everlasting and responsive soul!

17 you will not find me where emotional tempests rage, or while sensual storms bring turmoil and disquiet, first subdue these, for I await beyond, in the quietness of calm waters,

18 I must be sought as a lover seeks a loved one, in solitude, amid quietness and tranquillity, only there will I respond to the awakening kiss of recognition;

19 do not neglect me, O my beloved, or tarnish me, for I come to you as an inestimable treasure,

20 I bring beauty and innocence, gaiety and wholesomeness, decency and consideration, a jewel of potential perfection,

21 do not drag me down with you into the demon-haunted regions of darkness and terror!

22 I am yours, closer to you than any loved one of Earth,

23 if you spurn me, I go down to a terrible doom in darkness, there to be purged and purified from the corruption of your touch,

24 I am the sublime vehicle, awaiting the command to bear your true self to its destiny of glory! could anyone be so foolhardy as not to cherish me?

25 without moving, I am swifter than thought, on celestial wings I far outstrip the range of mortal senses,

26 I drink at the Fountain of Life and feed on the fruits of Eternal energy!

27 what are you, my beloved, but a passing thing fashioned of clay? a handful of dust given life by a spark from the Everlasting Flame?

28 I, myself, am no more than potential,

29 yet together, we are so great that Earth of itself alone cannot contain us! we transcend it to reach out into the realms of Divinity!

30 take me, awaken me, acknowledge me, cherish me, and I will carry you to realms of glory unimaginable on Earth!

31 behold, I am the imprisoned captive longing for return to the freedom of the Infinite, yet, because of my mortal love, I feel heart pangs of sorrow for things that pass away,

32 but I know that beyond the pains inseparable from a sojourn in the vale of tears, there shines a glorious rainbow of hope and joy,

33 there is a place of abiding love centred on the Infinite, there, if you will but cherish me, we shall not be denied expression!

34 man sees glory by the reflected light of glory within him, he knows love by the love within himself,

35 the sun is seen by the light of the sun, man sees the ruach by the light of the Ruach, and not by any light within his mortal self,

36 only by the light of the Ruach can the ruach of man be lit!

37 I am drawn by the Torah of Ruach-ual Gravitation towards union with the Universal Soul, and can no more escape return There than the mortal elements of man can escape their return to dust,

38 I delight in communion with the Great, with which I am akin, I rejoice in union with the Divine Ruach from whence I came!

39 I am at shalom when awakened to communion with my Adonai!

40 I am joyful when enthroned in consciousness! and when endowed with wisdom and vision transcending that of Earth!

41 I am your own true self, which should be forever cherished,

42 by listening to my whispers, by letting your thoughts dwell on me and by knowing me, the whole glory of the Greater is opened unto you,

43 I am that which reads what the eye sees, understands what the ear hears, knows what the hand feels, tastes whatever enters the mouth, and smells whatever is borne on the nose,

44 I am the indwelling consciousness which knows and enjoys all the good things of Earth!

45 those who dwell in the darkness of delusion cannot know me, and to them is lost the greatest joys of life,

46 all conceptions of beauty, love, and kindness are due to the consciousness residing in me,

47 when I depart from my earthly abode, I will carry with me the knowledge of the senses as the wind carries perfume from the

flower, or stench from a tannery,

48 I am not born, nor will I ever die, once awakened to an existence in consciousness, I can never become nothingness,

49 I am the everlasting one who dies not when life departs from the body!

50 O call me forth! awaken me from sleep with the kiss bestowing conscious life,

51 let me not lie unnoticed, wrapped in the heavy mantle of perpetual slumber, dreamless, unknowing!

52 I am the indestructible one! fire cannot burn me, swords cannot maim me, or water smother me;

53 when a drum is beaten, the sound it gives forth cannot be grasped or held, as that sound, so am I,

54 when a shell is blown, the note it gives forth cannot be grasped or held, as that note, so am I,

55 when a pipe is played, the music it gives forth cannot be grasped or held, as that music, so am I;

56 I am the immaterial in the material awaiting recognition, but in my own sphere, I am the substantial one, there, man-known matter is no more substantial than the dawn mists are here,

57 I am the fire of life in all things that breathe, and in union with the breath, I consume the nourishing substance within the food which feeds the body,

58 I am the kernel within the seed in the heart,

59 I am the guardian of memory, and the arbiter of wisdom;

60 these things are mine and ever with me, they are to me what the bones and muscles are to the mortal body:

61 The waking and sleeping consciousness, the awareness of self, the powers of feeling and of activity, and the controlling ruach, which is the sensitive being;

62 I am the living consciousness within you, I am the knower,

63 the things seen by the eye and the things smelt by the nose are received by me, the things heard and the things felt are registered by me,

64 I am the inner being causing all decisions to be made,

65 the tongue reports back outside the things, that I, the soul, hold recorded,

66 everything done and undertaken, such as the working of the hands and movement of the legs, all are done in accordance with my command,

67 when I depart, the body without me is as useless as a worn-out garment which is discarded and cast aside;

68 when we depart, will we go together, my beloved, hand in hand as lovers?

69 do I return home radiant in the pride of blooming consciousness? or, spurned and humiliated, return without sensitivity, memory, or knowledge?

70 do I return to be welcomed with joy in the light of glory? or, must I shamefully seek refuge in the darkness?

71 I am yours, my beloved, do with me as you will.

Chapter 16

1 When the shadowy form of the grim one beckons you to the Dark Portal, do not bewail the hour of his coming,

2 in due course, he comes to all, and carries the young as well as the aged,

3 the welcome you have prepared yourself, what have you to fear?

4 fear not death! for when he comes, you will be no longer there,

5 nevertheless, it is well to live a good life and be free from the fear of his shadow,

6 for he that is good has nothing to fear!

7 what is death but the gateway to glory? the entrance into the Kingdom of Greater Life?

8 it is a journey to a new land, an awakening from a sleep, where all care and affliction borne on Earth are left behind! selah;

9 while there is but one way of entry into life, there are a thousand ways of departing,

10 all roads through life lead to the gates of death,

11 the deer does not cry until it feels the arrow, nor does the fowl shriek until the hunting hound seizes it,

12 but he who ever dwells under the shadow of the fear of death dies many times, and the fear is greater than the event itself,

13 death I fear not!

14 if violent men come with sharp weapons as its messenger, I may fear the instruments,

15 I may fear dying, but death itself holds no terrors, come it must,

16 of all things in life it is the most inevitable,

17 Great Adonai, grant I accept it as a man.

The Lived Religion - Book 4 - The Man of Elohim

Chapter 1

1 Man is divided not only into nations, peoples, tribes, and creeds, but also broadly in twain:

2 There are among all men, all peoples, two kinds of man: The Man of Elohim, and the weakling;

3 those who are neither wholly one, nor wholly the other, nevertheless, tend towards the nature of one or the other of these;

4 consider the Man of Elohim: He is the man who reaches out towards elohim-liness,

5 he is the man in whom Elohim has succeeded, he is Elohim's elect!

6 he is like unto a spreading tree planted in black soil which blossoms quietly and doubles the yield of its fruit in the summer,

7 its fruit is a delight to the mouth and fills the stomach with satisfaction,

8 beneath the canopy of its foliage the weary find a pleasant refuge from the heat, in its shade all men find shalom and contentment;

9 behold the uprightness of the Man of Elohim:

10 Is he not the father of the orphan? and the husband of the widow? the brother of the forsaken? and the guardian of the fatherless?

11 do not the friendless find in him a friend? and the poor a benefactor?

12 it is not hard to give to the needy within reach or to help the weak when they are at hand,

13 but the Man of Elohim works not in such narrow confines, for he stretches out his hand to those beyond,

14 watch him among the distressed, as he talks with compassion and listens with understanding, see him among the lowly, how he deals with them in patience and kindness,

15 such men stand out, not only because of their own qualities, but because of the respect which others feel bound to accord them!

16 the Man of Elohim remains unperturbed by the whims of life,

17 he does not flinch before misfortune, or, turn his head when fortune smiles upon him,

18 when misfortune descends upon him, and his hopes and dreams are shattered, he does not go about lamenting in a loud voice, but quietly continues his daily task,

19 if fortune is gracious towards him, he braces himself and is not overwhelmed,

20 for he knows that often it takes a better man to bear the bounty of fortune than to bear the burden of misfortune!

21 the ruach of the Man of Elohim does not bow before the blows of misfortune, no matter how grievous its afflictions,

22 his calmness deflects its arrows, and his fortitude breaks its

thrust, the shield of cheerfulness and the sword of courage, he never discards in despair,

23 he has compassion on the blind man, he helps the lame man, and he guards the deformed and afflicted against the mockery of weaklings,

24 he carries himself with the dignity becoming a man! he remains unshaken in calamity,

25 deceit and hypocrisy are things far beneath him, he has an air of quiet confidence and courage to speak the Truth,

26 the thoughts of his heart are the words of his mouth, and whatever he promises is as good as done!

27 the Man of Elohim is he who serves the Purpose of Elohim and carries out His Plan,

28 because of him, all men rejoice for what they are, and the weakling he carries as his burden,

29 he treasures womanhood and the dreams of men,

30 he is the master of Earth, and the adon of creation!

31 nothing more is required of man on Earth than that he be a Man of Elohim,

32 this is a sufficient objective, and difficult enough for any man to achieve.

Chapter 2

1 Manhood is a state of freedom! but its stronghold is in the ruach

of a man,

2 the body may be held forcibly in bondage, but the ruach cannot be shackled!

3 he who lies imprisoned in the lowest dungeon may be more free than he who walks above, with a servile ruach holding him in thraldom;

4 be not a loud-mouthed bag of wind, for quietness within a man is as a rock,

5 against which, the tempest-driven waves of wrath and rage, rashness and haste, dash in vain;

6 only the Men of Elohim, can, with safety, destroy the tangled forests and wilderness of Earth, and make from them gardens, but will those who till the gardens be real men?

7 the Torah decrees that they must be, or the wilderness will reclaim its own!

8 he who would live in a garden must labour in the sun and subdue the soil,

9 he who is content to live in the wilderness may sleep in the shade, but he is a slave of life;

10 the Man of Elohim stands out above all others, his head is high, his footfall firm,

11 his bearing is dignified, his face calm, his hand steady, his heart tranquil, he sweeps aside all obstacles in his way,

12 he proceeds through all the dream fiends and powers of darkness that seek to bar his progress!

13 but where today is he who can gather the Men of Elohim together? and make them rulers of all men! that Earth may resound with glory and greatness?

14 the burden of the Man of Elohim and the shame of the Earth, is the weakling: He is one that frustrates the Plan of Elohim and degrades all men,

15 the weakling is wicked of heart, for wickedness comes easily to men,

16 it is easier to be wicked than to be good, it is easier to be weak than to be strong,

17 the weakling is one who takes the easy path;

18 the soul of the wicked man is wrapped in a winding sheet of hate, and corruption eats his ruach,

19 he mocks, for mockery is an overspill of poison brewed in little hearts;

20 the Man of Elohim would rather be hated than mocked, for while men hate, cowards mock;

21 man is divided in twain: Men of Elohim and weaklings; take your place with one or the other, for they will never be reconciled!

Chapter 3

1 Lend your arm to the aged, and open your purse at the cry of the poor,

2 guard well against the urge to plunder the unprotected, and from treating the destitute with harshness,

3 if you are lacking in compassion for others, it is well to remember that today one man may be rich and another poor,

4 yet ere a year has passed, the rich man may be working in a stable, and the poor man may be clothed in fine linen, such are the balances of life,

5 and it is therefore wise to turn a like countenance towards all men;

6 do not deride the clumsy speech of a lowly man,

7 the pleasant phrases of the pretentious man may be pretty things of no substance, sincerity is rarely bedecked with finery,

8 what a man has in his head and heart is more important than the fine words that fall from his lips;

9 an honest man is slow of speech, he fumbles for words and is confused, but his eye is straight,

10 the wily man is quick of speech, his wits are ever sharp from constant use;

11 if any man, himself being powerful, defrauds the helpless, he shall be your enemy! nor shall he be your enemy in secret, for this would make you a hypocrite,

12 if you see injustice, hide it not in your heart, but cry it from the housetops!

13 the Man of Elohim is the protector of the unprotected and counsellor of the ignorant,

14 for there will always be those who abuse power and strength to oppress,

15 they will rob the poor, oppress the afflicted, exploit the helpless man, and seduce the ignorant maiden from the household of her father,

16 they burden the Earth! and the Man of Elohim knows how to deal with them;

17 manliness carries its burden of responsibility, it is not a gown of fine linen, but a coat of mail,

18 it is not sufficient for the Man of Elohim that he turn away from wickedness, a Man of Elohim is called to enter the fight! and his instructions are to combat evil wherever he finds it,

19 he who sees an evildoer at work and remains silent is an accomplice!

20 he who remains inactive in the presence of evil condones the deed!

21 that which is not actively opposed is encouraged! take hold of yourself, be a man!

22 though now you have a body given over to weaknesses, the soul within has a reserve of resolution, call it forth, and it will serve you well!

Chapter 4

1 Forget the things wherein you are strong, for they need no attention,

2 consider your weaknesses and failings and keep them ever in sight;

3 beware the weakness of indecision, for at times a bad decision is better than no decision at all,

4 I say, beware of irresolution, as sometimes better is it to journey along the wrong path than never to start;

5 set out a code of conduct peculiar to yourself and at all times abide by it,

6 never betray the principles you set yourself, and thus, you will find the road to stability,

7 he who has no rules to abide by is like a vessel which has lost its steering oar, or as an unmanned chariot;

8 suppress the desires that rise to dominate you! selah;

9 relinquish the urges that drive to misfortune, and the shalom reigning within will not be disturbed by anxiety and disappointment,

10 away from the beguilement of false womanhood! from the tables of intemperance and the sideboards of gluttony!

11 go, seek your place in the company of Men of Elohim! see, are they not upstanding, brave, and active?

12 they are surrounded by the halo of vigour, they vibrate with the song of vitality, their arms are brawny and strong, and labour is to them as play to the child,

13 their talk is virile and manly, they know the weaknesses of

fornicators and the softness of she-men,

14 their passions are vanquished by self-command, and evil habits do not suck their ruchot,

15 they take their pleasures in moderation, and therefore the enjoyment endures!

16 their hours of shabbat are few, but their sleep is deep and sound,

17 their hearts are serene and their bodies strong,

18 their thoughts are quick and their form lithe,

19 they are men, and the sons of men.

Chapter 5

1 Rejoice, O man, in your body's strength and cleanliness, be not ashamed of your nature,

2 live in shalom and contentment, for cakes of flour and water eaten with a contented heart serve the body better than fine meats eaten with strife and enmity;

3 courage is not the absence of fear, but the conquest of fear, fear comes to the courageous and cowardly alike,

4 the greatest courage is that which cheerfully and stoutly fights a losing battle!

5 at all times, whatever the circumstances, bear yourself manfully, with courage and fortitude!

6 set an example to others by ever reaching out to the limits of your capabilities,

7 let your arm be ever ready to guard the unprotected, ease the plight of the destitute, and turn not your face from the misery of the hungry!

8 if you turn a hungry man away unsatisfied, and he steal to satisfy the craving within his belly, how can you, who are well fed, judge him? and expect to be held guiltless before Adonai?

9 it is not the way of a Man of Elohim to defile the house of another in his absence,

10 only weaklings sneak around furtively to gratify their body lust in another's domain;

11 strive always to be the best in your calling, whatever it may be, and let not your energy be consumed in the envy of another's achievements,

12 strive always to improve your own abilities, so that you may take your place among the masters of your craft;

13 seek not to take advantage of your competitor by any underhanded methods,

14 but overcome his opposition only through your own superiority, thus, even though you may fail, the blow will be softened by the retention of your honour;

15 all labour is vain unless done with purpose, and toil should not only be to sustain the body but also to satisfy the ruach,

16 the man who attacks the task with zest shows his love of life!

17 if you toil without satisfaction, if you labour with distaste, following a dull routine of drabness, then it were better you did not labour at all,

18 a loaf baked with indifference sits heavily on the stomach,

19 if a dwelling is built without care, it becomes a home to discomfort,

20 do good wherever you can and labour to the best of your ability, and gladness shall rule your heart!

21 toil is more your lot on Earth than revelation, speculation about Divine things need not extend beyond the confines of your heart,

22 keep the desires of your heart ever within moderation, and they will come to fruition in due course!

23 never let another excel you in goodness,

24 and never envy another his abilities, for such is a profitless thing, seek rather to improve your own;

25 never seek to further your plans by unworthy or mean methods, or to pull another down that you may rise above him,

26 seek only to reach your goal by virtue of your own superiority, and if success elude you, nevertheless honour will walk at your side;

27 honesty does not necessarily bring its own reward on Earth,

28 the true reward of honesty is the unperceptible strengthening of the soul,

29 Men of Elohim are honest for the sake of honesty, it is in their nature,

30 weaklings are hypocritically honest, because of the reward reaped for a reputation for honesty, only the Ruach is not deceived!

31 maintain your self-control at all times,

32 the fires of fanaticism burn strongly and consume reason, therefore, dampen down the heated thoughts which burn in a fervent heart,

33 the man who walks slowly often finds the quickest way;

34 he who leads to victory is great, but he who can lead in defeat is still greater,

35 the Man of Elohim is seen at his best in defeat.

The Lived Religion - Book 5 - The Fool

Chapter 1

1 The existence of a Supreme Being is not just something to accept, believe in, and ignore!

2 a belief, faith alone, cannot be ends in themselves, for nothing exists without purpose,

3 simple belief is not enough! we must know the purpose or intention of the Being,

4 if we believe this Supreme Being created us, however this was brought about, we must seek to discover the reason behind our creation,

5 if we were created to serve some purpose, to do something we were intended to do, we must do it or earn our Creator's displeasure!

6 does the potter make a pot but not use it for its purpose? or the smith keep unwrought metal?

7 only things which serve the purpose for which they were intended are kept and cherished,

8 each man is a supporting pillar of the House of Elohim, if the pillars be rotten, the roof crashes;

9 Truth is not a quality of Earth, but an infusion from the Greater Region beyond the veil, where it is manifested in purity,

10 here on Earth, things do not disclose their true nature to the eye, for the things we see with the eye are not as they are in

Reality and Truth, the eye is often a poor interpreter of Reality!

11 to attain Truth, man must reach out beyond Earth and himself,

12 while he remains bound to Earth, he may perceive the light of Truth only dimly in its reflection from the Source afar,

13 nevertheless, to strive for Truth must be one of the main aims of a man's life,

14 therefore, Earth teaches man the nature of deceit and places it all about him! that he may observe its ways, and learn to distinguish its illusions, selah;

15 life is in the nature of a game, wherein man tries to discover what is Reality, so far with little success,

16 for the road to Truth lies through the thick forests of illusion, and across the wide wastelands of deceit;

17 your responsibilities will beset your life with care, and the road you journey is stony and encompassed with pitfalls and thorns,

18 the cup you drink will seem more often bitter than sweet,

19 earthly success is not the measure of a man's achievement, and an earthly loss may mean a ruach-ual gain,

20 the scales are always just!

21 unlock the secrets of a stone and perchance you will find a star! open the body of water and you may discover a heart of fire!

22 then with regard to Truth and falsehood, do they not appear alike in things beyond our understanding?

23 how then could we decide between them? were it not for our soul hearing the whisper of the Ruach?

Chapter 2

1 For you, the best Scripture is the one which benefits you the most,

2 in one Scroll, Truth may be described in one way, and in another Scroll it may be described differently, but this need not mean that one is right and the other wrong,

3 Truth never goes unveiled, but the wise man seeks her where she is veiled the least!

4 general opinion is the least proof of Truth, for men in general are ignorant,

5 though man may realise their surroundings and circumstances on Earth are more conducive to deception than to Truth, few know that this is so for the benefit of man;

6 the wise man seeks after Truth, for it is the greatest of things a man can understand! Elohim's nature is beyond his comprehension, but Truth is not,

7 progress through life is Truth's unveiling, selah; but can man ever stand in her august presence?

8 it alone is the path towards the fulfilment of the destiny of man!

9 the weakling and unworthy man says, "What have I to do with Truth? which too often breeds wrath and stirs up trouble?

10 is not the soft word more desirable? and is that not the

password to popularity?"

11 weakling and fool! are not the foes made by Truth better than the friends made by falsehood?

12 those who seek Me are men becoming more than men, they are treading the road to elohim-hood!

13 know that those who close their minds to the Truth, are actually closing the doors of their own cage, in which they will live as little more than a beast,

14 therefore walk always towards Truth! and though it will recede as you approach, for it is unattainable on Earth, nevertheless, you are proceeding in the right direction,

15 Truth alone can set men free,

16 for great Truths are the food of the soul, and great souls are the inheritors of Eternity!

17 the day will come when I can speak to man openly about his real nature and destiny,

18 and in that day his ruach will respond and unfold its glory like a flower bud opening to the sun!

19 in that day, he will accept that the change called death is but the port of departure to a greater realm of activity,

20 he will then understand what he really is, and must become, to fulfil his destiny!

Chapter 3

1 Friends, when in old age you say, "Alas that life is short!" then consider the way you abused and wasted it in your youth, is not your reward fitting?

2 remember that the paths to pleasant old age are chosen in youth: They are the paths of simplicity, moderation, cleanliness, and virtue;

3 is it not economy which makes a servant of Adonai rich? and not abundance?

4 therefore, the Great Adonai in His wisdom has ordained the proper span of man's life,

5 yet, still you think that life is short? so why dissipate it so? why waste the precious days in sluggishness? or acts of folly?

6 the wise man lives fully all his life, and he is always conscious of being alive!

7 the fool is always beginning to live, and the weakling shrinks from life and seeks forgetfulness in comfort,

8 those who half live are already half dead!

9 there are some men who seek the light to a point, but will go so far, and no further,

10 declaring the life they found is not the one they sought, and fall back into the dark, losing what little light they did find,

11 yet if a man seek gold and find silver, does he throw it away? better half a loaf than no loaf at all;

12 if gold were as plentiful as copper, it would be valued less than silver, only the things hard to obtain have value,

13 and what is more difficult to discover than Eternal Truth! which must be sought beyond the boundaries of Earth?

14 only the beginning of the long road towards it is here, and it is this beginning you must seek;

15 every journey has a beginning and an end, and you can make your way only in one direction,

16 if you are dispirited, be comforted by the knowledge that you need only find the beginning of the road, then, having found it, let every step you take be along it,

17 the journey is long and the road rough and stony, but do not turn back before you find the first staging post, you will acquire from the Ruach new strength and encouragement there!

18 if we have difficulties among the worldly men, the difficulties among ourselves are no less! the Truth we have seems not only unpalatable, but also indigestible,

19 men seek tastier food, even though it is less sustaining, and few replace the brothers who depart,

20 would we serve the Great Adonai better if we presented Truth as a draught diluted with water?

21 companions in suffering, raise your heads and cease your lament! misery and sorrow, trial and tribulation are the appointed lot of man,

22 there are no shortage of challenges to the man living in Truth,

23 Great Adonai, let the tests not be beyond our endurance.

Chapter 4

1 Men sit beneath trees and nod their heads solemnly and roll out long books to read things that evaporate in the air,

2 I deride not the books, but one blow of the sword can destroy ten thousand strokes of the pen;

3 those in high places persecute us, not because of the Words of the Scriptures, for that much is common to all, but because we seek to change the established order of things,

4 we seek to change the ever-present state of affairs,

5 because, too, we have an Adonai who is not the holder of property, or an Elohim of the rich and powerful,

6 who benefits from the riches and estates of other elohim? the elohim? or their priests?

7 would they who benefit, therefore welcome the Words of the True Elohim? such is not the nature of men,

8 and we have the nigh impossible task of changing the natures of men!

9 it is true that we may keep the Truth as we find it, if a man seek for unwrought gold and find it, he has not made it, yet it is still his,

10 is it not also written, "Gold is the treasure of a lifetime, but Truth is the treasure of Eternity?"

11 gold can nourish the body, but it may poison the soul,

12 yet the coming of riches is not a misfortune and the inheritance of estates is not a calamity to the wise man, for he will utilise them with temperance and discretion;

13 life is yours! selah; that you requested it not is of small consideration, for the choice was not with you,

14 therefore accept with good grace that which has been allotted to you, deriving from it whatever benefits it may bestow!

15 keep forever the joys of friendships well made, and serve your friends well,

16 never betray friendship or turn it to serve your own ends, lest you become something less than a man;

17 carry high gladness in your heart, and never cease to wonder at the marvels in life!

18 not a day shall pass, but you will see something new to enrich your thoughts,

19 look at life as a man and not as an ox, wonder at the great and awesome manifestations of Adon!

20 such as sunlight and thunder, the dew and the stars, the sandstorm and the murmur of waters,

21 never let your eyes become dulled to the growth of trees, to the rising of the waters, and to the return of the harvests!

22 consider the extent of your own patience and forbearance, has your temper been tested in fires of provocation?

23 remain passive when the waves of passion seethe within you, the wise captain remains in harbour during the violence of the

storm;

24 let your heart be hungry for knowledge, and your hand be ever seeking some skill,
25 hate lies, and shun the coward,

26 walk with men, and learn manly ways.

Chapter 5

1 The Kodesh Words of Truth remain with us, but are they lightly regarded by those who should cherish them?

2 few still walk in their light, and in all the land the right way of life is avoided and the path of righteousness is spurned, is it beyond the strength of men today?

3 wisdom is the treasure of all ages, which shall endure incorruptibly forever until time is spent!

4 therefore, let the tumult of life be stilled, and in reverence and silence receive these instructions from ancient times,

5 my brothers, listen to the voice of the Instructing Ruach and incline a willing ear towards the speech of wisdom!

6 thus shall the words which issue from your mouth be established before men, and you will never lack for shalom,

7 let not your mind be diverted, nor your attention be distracted,

8 set them in your heart, inscribe them there as though struck on marble,

9 to cast aside the words of experience which guided the ancients

is foolhardy and an invitation to calamity!

10 therefore, immerse yourself in the writings of the past, as in cool waters at the heat of the day, and your ruach will emerge refreshed and strengthened!

11 they will be a steadying oar, enabling the vessel of your heart's desire to alter course without capsizing!

12 you will learn the first step towards being wise is to acknowledge the extent of your ignorance,

13 concern yourself with the vast amount of knowledge that you lack, and place no undue importance on what little knowledge you do possess,

14 as womanly loveliness is best displayed in a modest garment, so is modest behaviour and unpretentious bearing best becoming the wise,

15 remember that all men are born equally into ignorance, yet no man, whatever his estate, lacks the means to acquire wisdom and Truth,

16 for true wisdom comes not from books and instruction, but from observation and enquiry,

17 the learned scribe knows a thousand books, but what knows he about the ways of the grasshopper?

18 the earthly life of a man depends not on his knowledge of books, but on his knowledge of the Earth, but better still to have knowledge of the Ruach!

19 if you would not be deemed foolish in the eyes of others, then cast aside the desire to appear wise to your own edification,

20 if you try to appear wise among the foolish, then you will appear foolish among the wise!

21 if wisdom now be held in low esteem, it is not wisdom's loss, but man's!

22 wisdom cries outside the palace and the hovel, she is heard in the streets, and in the gathering places,

23 her voice says, "O fools and sons of fools! how long will you delight in your foolishness?"

24 but the pleasure of fools is in their foolishness, and the pleasure of the weak is in their own weakness, and therefore, they scorn the voice of wisdom,

25 yet this I say unto you, the mockers of the wise and the scorners of wisdom shall tomorrow be forgotten,

26 and the wisdom they deride shall have its day! when they are dust and their names forgotten,

27 let the fool eat of his tree, it will provide no sustenance in times of evil,

28 when the whirlwind sweeps across the face of the land, bringing destruction in its wake, fools will be swallowed up, and Earth will be as if they had never been.

Chapter 6

1 He who has grown to wisdom never acts but at wisdom's command!

2 to some has been granted the ability to soak up wisdom, as the sand soaks up water,

3 if this be your gift from Elohim, then hug it not to your own breast as would the mean man,

4 share it with those who are less wise for their instruction, and hide it not from the wise, for they will multiply it;

5 the wise man is less presumptuous than the fool,

6 he has many doubts and changes his mind, for as wisdom grows, knowledge alters,

7 the fool fixes his mind in obstinacy, he is stubborn, and doubt does not disturb his placidity, he knows all things, except his own ignorance;

8 the wise man is aware of his imperfections and continually strives for improvement,

9 the fool forever counts his own small talents and is content, he boasts of his achievements in things which are of no account,

10 thistledown floats on water for all to see, but a gemstone sinks below the surface,

11 so does the fool shout his abilities to the wind, while a wise man keeps them hidden within himself;

12 the goose brings forth its egg while at rest, and the tail of the peacock is displayed while it stands still,

13 the deep, still pool holds the biggest fish, and the resting cow gives the most milk,

14 so it is with the shalom-ful man, who within himself produces a fountain of strength at which other men drink, finding refreshment and courage;

15 the heart of a fool flutters at a vain hope, but the wise man puts it behind him,

16 fools snap at one another, but wise men disagree in shalom,

17 the wise man does not need advice, and the fool will not take it,

18 rebuke a fool and he will dislike you, rebuke the wise and they will hold you in regard;

19 the fool does right in his own eyes, he justifies his deeds with a loud mouth,

20 when you have nothing to say, say nothing, never lash the air with your tongue,

21 he who speaks for the sake of hearing his own voice has an audience of one, and that a fool!

22 be not like the wagging-tongued man, an unbridled horse is difficult to control;

23 open not your ears to tales of your neighbour's doings, can you think of no better things?

24 give ear to nothing but that which lies within the orbit of your own interests,

25 repeat not the words of another, unless for a useful purpose!

26 a tongue has been given you and the power of speech, use

these, the powers that distinguish you from the beast,

27 to teach your children wisdom, and to discover for yourself the way of Truth.

Chapter 7

1 Let your tongue spread no report except of that which is good, reserving details of wickedness within yourself,

2 let the ears collect all that is spoken, the heart filter the good from the bad, and the mouth pour forth only that which is beneficial;

3 the abode of the wise man is a sanctuary against despair, a fortress against the forces of discontent,

4 his presence is as the gloom-dispelling sunlight, and his lips as the doors of a treasure house, they open, and gems pour forth;

5 whatever your store of wisdom, be prudent, let your heart serve as a counterbalance for your tongue,

6 let your lips speak true, your eye see only that which is right for it to see, and ensure that both your ears hear the same thing,

7 always be ready to heed advice and to accept instruction, bearing in mind that it is more profitable to listen than to speak,

8 while good counsel is always carefully considered by the wise, fools brush it aside,

9 what a fool wants to believe, he will;

10 a wise man knows his limitations and seeks the advice of

others, and if the advice is good, what matters who gives it?

11 advice is either good or bad, irrespective of who gives it,

12 accept advice that is helpful, even though it may not be palatable,

13 good counsel can come forth from the mouth of a fool, and bad counsel from the mouth of the wise,

14 even the wisest of men will do foolish things, and everything said and done by a fool is not folly;

15 the man who thinks himself wise believes nothing until it is proven to him, but the wise man considers everything possible until it is disproved;

16 never disdain the opinions of another, or condemn them because they differ from yours, might you not be wrong?

17 seek the company of those who are your superiors in wisdom, skill, and ruach-uality, that they may support you, and you will be raised up to prosper;

18 success is the child of diligence and persistence! it follows the footsteps of the wise, even as failure dogs the foolish,

19 men have the choice of either success or ease, they cannot have both!

20 a man who can be satisfied with little is the possessor of wisdom, he who desires no more than sufficient will always have enough, his cares will be few;

21 the powers of the Ruach enter into a man as a guest, it will not come unbidden or remain unwelcome,

22 wisdom cannot enter a heart whose gates are barred with prejudice, nor penetrate a body filled with evil,

23 wisdom concerns itself only with the things which are knowable, in matters that are to you forever unknowable, forbearance is wise,

24 wisdom is the fruit of past experience preserved for the future! the taste may be unappetising, but it can still nourish a healthy ruach, the fool who fasts from wisdom starves his soul;

25 let your aim be to live as long as you should, and not as long as you can,

26 while to others your life is worth more than death, then your duty is to preserve it, while you serve best by living, live,

27 but when by your death the living may best be served, then shirk not the burden of manhood;

28 to be beaten and still not surrender, that is true victory!

29 that which accords with the Plan of Elohim and benefits man is good, so, that which is against the welfare of man is evil,

30 but who among men is wise enough to discern what is good and what is evil?

31 therefore, inscribe the writings of wisdom on your heart, that you never lack a guide,

32 these are words which you will do well to absorb, as the dry sands soak up water!

33 though a man read only words of wisdom, they are useless

unless that man has control over himself,

34 they also have no value to a heart which is unable to feel compassion for others,

35 or to fools, who close their ears to the Truth.

The Lived Religion - Book 6 - Earth

Chapter 1

1 In ruach-ual matters, the most important step is that each man should awaken his own soul,

2 a task far more difficult than it may appear, but a task for which Earth is the dedicated instrument,

3 the first objective to attain towards this end is self-taming,

4 just as a horse has to be broken in before it can be of any service, so has the mortal body of man to be tamed and brought under control,

5 to do this requires not only self-discipline, but also the ability to rise above earthly conditions, no easy task,

6 for Earth is a hard taskmaster and a worthy adversary, and the mortal body of man an unruly steed;

7 brothers in belief, there are two roads through life: The road of good and the road of evil,

8 they are not clearly defined roads, and often run side by side and sometimes cross each other,

9 those who travel without a guide, or in darkness, often mistake one road for the other,

10 it is the dark night of wickedness when ignorance covers the Earth,

11 yet though the pillars of Heaven fall and though the great

abyss open, the Earth shall not end until its purpose is fulfilled!

12 look in the places of judgment: They are filled with low people, and unclean feet rest upon the footstools,

13 priests grow fat on riches bestowed for the preservation of the body, while those who speak of the preservation of the soul are tormented,

14 men talk of the fleeting delights of life, but who cares for the Eternal life of the ruach?

15 the voice of the people cries out for the blood of the wise, and upon their heads blood shall be!

16 it is a time of sorrow, it is a time of distress, it is a time of tribulation, this is no new thing,

17 for the darkness of ignorance has often preceded the brighter days of ruach-ual awakening,

18 but we who dwell under the shadow of darkness see nought but the sorrows of our times,

19 we are as carrion yet unseen by the vultures, or as a tomb laying open to the despoilers,

20 our doctrine is as a leprosy upon us, for the life of a man who cannot impart his knowledge to another is futile,

21 men live to learn, but also to teach,

22 though some brothers are not well equipped to instruct in earthly matters, and therefore should leave it to another, the caravan moves quicker when each man rides his own camel;

23 dark looks are cast upon those filled with the ancient wisdom,

24 the people's pleasure is with those who seek acclaim in lewdness!

25 then there are those who perform vain deeds of deceit,

26 when they perform some filthy deed, the people say, "This was the custom of our fathers, and our fathers' fathers before them, therefore, it is surely permitted before The One Adonai!"

27 men make plans, they are as nought, they are as words written on the waters, as commands given to the wind,

28 wise is he who knows the Plans of Elohim, for to them the whole Earth conforms.

Chapter 2

1 Men cry out at the tribulations of life, not knowing that by adversity alone can they find their soul,

2 they say, "Why are we beset with trial and tribulation?" for they cannot understand the contest,

3 they say, "Why must we seek and never find?" knowing not that life itself is the search! and at the end man will discover himself!

4 O man, gaze well upon the Earth, behold, is it not by its nature a place of labour? and not a garden of pleasure? or a panderer to your weaknesses?

5 Truth is found in the Kodesh Scriptures of Life, but may be understood by degrees,

6 for who among men receiving the whole would not be overwhelmed and destroyed?

7 in general, men are childlike, give the people deceitful things, and they will rejoice like children,

8 show them amusing things, and they will acclaim their pleasure,

9 the elohims of fear are held in reverence, but The Great Adonai Who banishes fear, they despise!

10 O foolish people! O foolish generation! with dust on my head I mourn your ignorance,

11 with loud lamentations I decry your folly! yet the path you have chosen, you have chosen freely,

12 ease and comfort appear to be your end and purpose!

13 the adonais of deceit have temples of splendour, their priests are well clothed and overfed,

14 but The Great Adonai of Truth has no more than a hidden cavern, His servants are garbed in rags, and their bellies are empty,

15 the elohims of lust and cruelty have storehouses of treasure, but The Elohim of Kindness has not even a field,

16 the people worship els that oppress, and ignore The El Who frees,

17 they give to the elohims that take, and spurn The Elohim Who gives! O misguided generation!

18 O blind and ignorant people, to cherish the stone adons of

death! and mock The Adon of Life!

19 O misguided generation, to clasp to its breast the things that inherit decay, and spurn the things that are Eternal!

Chapter 3

1 Things remain unchanged: The good suffer while the wicked prosper!

2 whose fault is this? certainly not El's, this is a man-made state,

3 it was built by strength, and strength must smash it down and rebuild,

4 the good have been too passive, arise from your knees and look the foe in the face!

5 be a man of fortitude and courage, prepared to fight, strike a blow for El and good!

6 there is work to be done in the Garden of Adonai,

7 therefore, cease useless performances and word-wasting discussions, go, pick up the hoe and tackle the task to hand!

8 the reason that there is so little Divine intervention is not that the Divine remains indifferent, but that man has been given all the powers and wisdom necessary to deal with the affairs of Earth,

9 if he fails to make use of them, who then is to blame?

10 the duty and obligation placed upon man relate to his reaching upward towards ruach-uality, and outward towards perfection,

11 if man declines to do this, he must accept the consequences, and can blame none but himself,

12 from the days of the ancients have been heard the lamentations of the woeful and disheartened, as they ask the winds,

13 "Where have we failed? why does the Elohim we pray to remain unresponsive?

14 in this, our generation, goodly men have been robbed of their estates by warlike strangers,

15 their possessions have been sold to provide earthly pleasure for those who revel in things of the Earth,

16 and their wives have even been ravaged by men who have studied the ways of weaponry!"

17 in their dire despair they seek to lay the blame upon Elohim, Who does not strike down the wrongdoers, and seemingly rewards those who are earthly wise,

18 "Wherein have we failed?" this is the echo in the corridors of the ages!

19 they have failed because they have left to Elohim, the things which they, as Elohim's overseers on Earth, should have accomplished!

20 it is men in the mass who permit evil to flourish in their midst,

21 their woeful lamentations ascend to Heaven and call upon the Heavenly Hosts for aid,

22 but better by far would it be were they to call upon their own resolution and fortitude, and fight the good fight! to bring about

the rule of right and justice!

23 all that is wrong with the Earth has its genesis in men, and if evil stalks the land, then it follows after the attitudes and acts of men,

24 therefore, it is men who must make recompense for their lack of concern,

25 if a nation establish the way of iniquity, then it is the wrongdoers who will be rewarded with bounty, and this is not Elohim's will but man's,

26 if the people lament and are disenchanted with the way things are, then it is a time for action rather than a time for prayer,

27 pray not for Heavenly help, but for a strong right arm! and righteous wrath and resolution!

28 the way of despair is for weaklings.

Chapter 4

1 Life on Earth is a treasure house of hidden things!

2 with so much mystery and beauty about them, why do hearts of men incline towards sordid things?

3 shalom brings glory and beauty to the soul, yet, can your soul be formed except by suffering?

4 can clay be made beautiful except through scars? can metal be fashioned to form except by fire?

5 we journey towards a light we cannot reach and fall into a pit of

darkness, to find the light at the bottom,

6 we gaze on the beauty of the stars and think them high above, when, behold, the light is within our hearts!

7 man is not born to play, but to labour,

8 life is a basket which must be filled with sustenance for the future,

9 the fool fills it with empty, unwholesome things, while the wise man fills it with things of lasting value;

10 man is born to live, but he is also born to die,

11 it is no more natural for him to live than it is for him to die, death is no more difficult than life!

12 the best of today is gone, we console ourselves that better will arise tomorrow,

13 each man will improve, or perish, that is the Torah!

14 forget not that life has but one purpose, one end, and one objective, and that is the awakening of the souls of men!

15 all things on Earth conform to that end,

16 Earth, without its perplexities and problems, its struggle and strife, its inequalities and injustices, would never develop the soul in a manner meet for its destiny,

17 this is the answer to the riddle of ages,

18 if all were right with the Earth, there would be nothing for man to do, as it is, there is sufficient to occupy him throughout his

generations,

19 when man himself is perfect, its purpose will be fulfilled, and then Earth, too, will be perfect!

Chapter 5

1 What is life that man should seek to prolong it?

2 is it not a continual avoidance of snares? a struggle against delusion? a series of mishaps? and a pursuit of shadows which retreat from the grasp?

3 it begins with ignorance, continues through strife and worry, and ends in sorrow and pain!

4 it is a day of heat, and death comes as a cool night;

5 life raises some men up and casts others down, not always does it bestow good fortune on the worthy or mete out to the unworthy their just desserts,

6 the reward of the worthy is not here, neither is the punishment of the wicked,

7 Earth raises men up to test them, and likewise, casts them down,

8 the man who discovers a golden treasure is being tested, even as he who is stricken with blindness,

9 each man is tested according to his weaknesses, not according to his strength;

10 every man is born to be tested and tried, sorrow and suffering, problems and tribulations, are meant to be the lot of men, selah;

11 yet they are never his continued lot, and the brighter moments of life far outweigh the darker!

12 man was not given life for the sole purpose of enjoying Earth and its pleasures,

13 Earth is a place man must cultivate and prepare for harvest, and what he produces will be his sustenance when the season is ended!

14 suffering and affliction are unavoidable if man is to develop into the elohim-like being intended!

15 he must grow ruach-ually strong, possessing both courage and compassion, and to do this he cannot be protected from suffering and affliction,

16 can the over-sheltered plant kept indoors withstand either the sun's heat or the windy blast?

17 however, it must be remembered that pain and suffering do not of themselves develop ruach-uality,

18 what is important is the manner in which they are endured, the ruach rising to the challenge, and the courageous conquest!

19 the suffering of each man should be an offering dedicated to the uplifting of mankind!

Chapter 6

1 I can add nothing to the Great Scripts in my keeping, for I am no more than a mere writing instrument,

2 no sublime thoughts arise in my heart, and I, who myself lack the strength of assurance, can scarce presume to impart it to others,

3 I serve as best I can, as a guardian and transmitter of the wisdom from olden times,

4 I labour in secret places, and I hide a secret life within my breast!

5 this is a miserable and misguided age,

6 when corruption stalks the land and the soul of man swims like a fish in an ocean of sin, and wallows like a pig in the mire and mud of lust,

7 it is a time of constant soul danger,

8 in this age of wickedness, neither good works, nor faith, nor ruach-ual wisdom have any value!

9 they who should instruct and guide the people mislead them with deceitful words and hypocritical ways,

10 they have become corrupt of heart, and their eyes are blind to their wrongdoing,

11 their deeds done in the name of righteousness are as the filth which pollutes pure waters,

12 the goodness that may once have bloomed within is withered away, and their ruchot are as shrunken and wrinkled husks!

13 the greed of the great is without bounds, and they oppress the poor beyond endurance,

14 they take away the milch goat of the fatherless and seize the widow's ass for debt,

15 in the Scripts of the Wise, it is said, "As a man sows, so shall he reap," but I seek vainly for its truth in this age,

16 is this beyond my understanding? yet, I shall pass on undiminished the treasure with which I have been entrusted,

17 let those with greater wisdom make of it what they will, it has proven poor fare for an empty stomach, and a cold covering for the lonely night,

18 yet it has brought its own strange consolation, and I am not without comfort;

19 think of me sometimes, when I am dust, and you are even as I am now,

20 if, in greater wisdom, you have solved the problems that now perplex me, look not upon me with scorn, for I am the child of my age,

21 meagre though my offering be, it extends to the limits of my capacity, more I cannot give.

The Lived Religion - Book 7 - Creation

Chapter 1

1 It is Elohim Whom I seek!

2 but how can I, a mere mortal, describe Him? only this do I know: Abba Adonai came into existence before all else,

3 He ever was, so none could know Him in the beginning, and none knows His nature,

4 as nothing came into existence before Him, how can I even name One Who had no father after Whom His Name might have been made?

5 none can display His likeness in writing, nor can it be cut with knife in wood or stone,

6 He is too great that men should even enquire about Him, with what words could He be described to their understanding?

7 He is the Almighty El! the Nameless One Whom your fathers held in awe!

8 all our hopes rest in this Elohim Supreme, Who created all things, sustaining them with His Breath, whatever their state,

9 wherever they may be in this place on Earth, or in any other place visible or invisible,

10 He alone causes herbs to blossom in beauty, and causes all things to come forth in their proper order and time! all things flow from His directing thoughts:

11 The shalom-ful beauty enfolding the face of the land at eventide,

12 the melody of song and speech, the fragrance of flowers, the soft delicacy of petal and wing,

13 all beauty and charm that delights the hearts of men, flow from Adon,

14 He is now, as in the beginning, and will be no different after the end! selah;

15 He formed men by building an earthly structure around a Heavenly Seed, and into this He infused the vapours of life,

16 He maintains the order of the Heavens and stabilises the land in the waters!

17 His Breath is the breath of life! and He causes water to fall and greenery to live!

18 look about you, and see Adon reflected as in a mirror, no mortal man has ever looked upon Him directly, but His reflection may be seen with immunity,

19 His wisdom is unbounded! and in His goodness He has provided all things in which He has created a need in man:

20 The daylight and wind, food and water, heat and coolness, the materials of his dwelling and the substance of his garments, all things for his daily use and enjoyment!

21 man lacks nothing which would increase his skill and knowledge, and to all useful things, guideposts have been planted along the way,

22 what need can man know for which Adon has not already made provision? even before man was born?

23 I established Truth as Eternal and unchanging!

24 the first Truth, which was in the beginning with Me, the Torah, will endure until the end, nothing can be added to it, and nothing taken away,

25 it may be viewed from many sides and appear different, but such differences are in the eyes of the beholders,

26 Truth itself is unalterable and cannot change!

27 Truth is not with man, nor of the Earth, it is with Me alone,

28 and when man sees Truth in its purity, he will see Elohim;

29 He has established the nature of all things, so they remain stable and come forth in their proper order without change,

30 when a man sows barley, he knows what will come up out of the ground, the rewards of his toil are not confusion,

31 a man lights a fire knowing it will cook his food, it is not sometimes hot and at other times cold,

32 he knows that day will follow night and that the hours of darkness are prescribed,

33 it is not a matter of chance, the hours of darkness are not one day long and the next day short,

34 oil is ordained for lamps and water to drink, man knows that he can not light a wick in water,

35 man looks about him and sees order, not confusion, and he knows that where there is organisation there must be an Organiser,

36 O, how I rejoice that Adon has made me as I am!

37 truly, He is in all and encompasses all, in His magnificence and majesty no man can conceive Him! for His Divine nature is beyond the understanding of man,

38 His creation is awesome! His ways unfathomable!

39 My love for My wayward children has been limitless and abounding!

40 it has remained changeless throughout the ages, fulfilling My Design,

41 I created, so that I might express and share My love, which is the very essence of My nature,

42 with beings created in My likeness! beings which could absorb and reflect that love!

43 yet, that My love might be wholly free, man was endowed with freewill, and freewill, man has used perversely!

Chapter 2

1 Eden was a fertile place, for out of the ground grew every kind of tree that was good for food, and every tree that was pleasant to the sight,

2 every herb that could be eaten and every herb that flowered was there,

3 the Tree of Life was within the Kodesh Enclosure,

4 there, too, was the Great Tree of Wisdom bearing the fruits of knowledge, granting the choice and ability to know the true from the false;

5 the fall severed man from The Source of his ruach-ual sustenance, thereafter his efforts were to struggle back,

6 in his blind groping for Adon after the fall, he discovered beings in the dark, and found it easier to worship them than to continue the search,

7 but He is always waiting, man has only to look up! but it is easier to go down the hill than to climb it,

8 it is easier for man's ruach-ual beliefs to degenerate than to evolve;

9 Who but the Greatest of Beings could have ordained your existence? Who but a Master Architect could have planned it?

10 how wonderfully you are made! how precise and perfect is the construction of your earthly habitation,

11 among all creatures, you alone stand erect, that you may enjoy and admire the wondrous works of your Creator, rejoice therefore in your form and in your body!

12 consider yourselves, my brothers, and meditate on the reason for your existence and the purpose for which He brought you into being,

13 contemplate your powers, ponder your circumstances, discover your inescapable duties, and face your earthly obligations!

14 each man is an individual work of Elohim, his mind a fragment of Elohim Himself! the Breath of Adon gives him life!

15 if it helps in your understanding, see The Supreme Elohim as a Being reflecting His image as yourself,

16 it is He Who fills Heaven and Earth with His might! and His powers are displayed in the elemental forces!

17 in olden times there were spawned great monsters and beasts in fearful form, with frightful gnashing teeth and long ripping claws,

18 an elephant was but a rat in comparison with them,

19 then, because of heavenly rebellion and turmoil, and the terror overwhelming the hearts of men,

20 the Great One hardened the face of the land, which had become unstable, and the beasts were changed to stone!

21 this was beforetimes, when the Destroyer still slumbered in the upper vaults of Heaven.

Chapter 3

1 The Supreme Elohim formed you as He fashioned the beasts of the field and forest, He made you last and placed you at the pinnacle of creation!

2 command and jurisdiction over all were given unto you,

3 from among the creatures of the forest and the beasts of the field you ascended in triumphant superiority, and your yoke is

upon them,

4 therefore, be aware of yourself as the pride of Adon, and the fruition of His Desire! nothing greater shall be created on Earth;

5 My child, you are the vessel containing the essence of Divinity, fashioned with the clay of matter,

6 behold, you have even the nature of Adon within you and partake of My substance,

7 remember therefore your superior estate, maintain the pride and dignity befitting your position, and descend not to any mean or degrading thing,

8 remember that every man, whatsoever his nation or estate, is a man, therefore never degrade anyone, for even the least among men contains a part of Me;

9 by a command He created man, and in His indulgence permitted the clay to be fashioned,

10 He is the Source of all that is, Abba Adonai, the One Who preceded the sun!

11 the sun is not Elohim, though His creation, for its brightness bestows light and life upon the Earth, it is the instrument of the High Adonai;

12 the sun is removed from man at night time, but the True Elohim is always with him, man never walks alone, he is never unescorted,

13 to this Adon alone give praise! Self-Created, Maker of Heaven and Earth! Founder of the Kingdoms of Light and Darkness, the Waters and the Mountains!

14 to the One that is above all! the Spring from which flows all wisdom, to Him alone belong adoration, thanksgiving, honour, and praise!

15 Who spread wide the great canopy of Heaven and pinned back the curtains of night with the stars!

16 Adam saw a vision of glory encompassing even the Realm of Splendour!

17 unbounded wisdom filled his heart, and he beheld beauty in perfection, the ultimates of Truth and Justice were unveiled before him,

18 he became one with the profound shalom of Eternity and knew the joys of unceasing gladness!

19 the Eternal ages of time unrolled as a scroll before his eyes, and he saw written thereon all that was to become and occur,

20 the great vaults of Heaven were opened up unto him, and he saw the everlasting fires and unconsumable powers that strove therein,

21 he felt within himself the stirring of inexpressible love, and unlimited designs of grandeur filled his thoughts,

22 his ruach ranged unhampered through all the realms of existence, he was then even as El Himself! and he knew the secret of all things,

23 then, I lifted My hand from man, and Adam was alone, the great vision departed and he awoke,

24 only a dim and elusive recollection, no more than the shadow

of a dream remained,

25 but deep within the sleeping soul there was a spark of remembrance, and it generated within Adam a restless longing for he knew not what,

26 henceforth, man was destined to wander discontented, seeking something he felt he knew but could not see,

27 something which continually eluded him, perpetually goaded him, and forever tantalised him,

28 deep within himself, man knew something greater than himself was always with him and part of him, spurring him on to greater deeds, greater thoughts, greater aspirations,

29 it was something out beyond himself, scarcely realised and never found,

30 something which told him that the radiance seen on the horizon, but dimly reflected the hidden glory beyond it!

Chapter 4

1 Behold the nature of man: Within him is a spark from the Divine Source, and this is the soul, the adonai of the body,

2 this alone is everlasting, this alone of man is his true self,

3 this spark is enwrapped within a heavy mantle of matter, it is enclosed in a covering of earthly clay,

4 this spark alone is the seat of life, it alone has understanding and thought,

5 such things are not with the clay of the flesh, neither are they kin to the stones from which the bones come,

6 the life within man radiates out from the enclosed spark, and through the blood, endows the body with life and heat,

7 life gives forth heat, and the greater the life, the greater the heat!

8 from The One comes the Kodesh Glow in its two aspects, which men call the Breath of Adon, and from this are made all things which are in Heaven and Earth,

9 as the sun gives light and fire spreads heat, as the flower radiates perfume, so does the Central Light give forth a vaporous unseeable glow, and this our fathers called the Breath of Adon,

10 this Breath comes forth in two manifestations: There is a heavy form and a light form, and from these all things are compounded;

11 behold, above is the Adon Adonai, and below Him are Heaven and Earth;

12 between Heaven and Earth, there is a great gulf across which the dwellers in Heaven may not return;

13 Heaven is divided in twain: There is a Place of Light and a Place of Darkness,

14 within the Place of Light dwell the ruchot of good and within the Place of Darkness dwell the ruchot of evil,

15 between them, the boundary is not fixed, but flows back and forth according to their fluctuating strengths,

16 but they who abide in the light shall always prevail! for light

will ever dispel darkness!

17 therefore, those who dwell in darkness withdraw before the brilliance of those who dwell in the light!

18 this light and darkness are not such as men can understand, for it is not the light and darkness known on Earth;

19 before the Gates of Heaven is the Land of the Horizon, whence go all who depart from their earthly body,

20 from here, there are two great gates: One leads to the Place of Light, and the other to the Place of Darkness,

21 and the soul of man is admitted into its appointed place according to its likeness:

22 He who is filled with the light cannot go to the Place of Darkness, for it would draw back before him,

23 neither can he who is a dark one go into the Place of Light,

24 for there, he would shrivel before the light, as the worm coming forth from the damp darkness of its hole shrivels in the light of the sun;

25 I am the Adon of Creation! and I hold the great waters within their appointed limits, the stormwater I keep in restraint!

26 I cover the face of the Earth with a green mantle of vegetation, I inundate the land with the waters of life!

27 My arm sweeps across the skies and men are bewildered, Earth is shaken, and nations collapse and fall!

28 the wicked tremble before My manifestations and are

consumed in the midst of My fire!

29 My voice speaks from the sandy silences, I whisper in the cool breezes,

30 I roar in the whirlwind and murmur in the running waters, I sigh in the treetops,

31 men hear My voice without understanding.

Chapter 5

1 Hearken to the voice of The Ruach of Elohim: I am the immortality latent in all things mortal, the light filling all things with radiance, the power holding all things to their form,

2 I am the pure invulnerable stream untouchable by evil, the supreme fountainhead of thoughts, the unfailing well of consciousness, the light of Eternity,

3 I am that to which the soul of man is related, I am its power, its life, its strength, I am that to which it responds,

4 I am the sweet coolness in refreshing waters and the comforting warmth in the sun,

5 I am the calmness of shalom in the radiance of the moon, and the delicacy in the moonbeam,

6 I am the sound heard in the stillness, the companionship felt in the solitude, the stirring in the hearts of men,

7 I am the cheerfulness in the laugh of a youth and the gentleness in the sigh of a maiden,

8 I am the joy in the life of all living things, and the content in the hearts of awakened souls,

9 I am the beauty in the beautiful and the fragrance in the fragrant, I am the sweetness in honey and the scent in perfume,

10 I am the power in the strong arm, and the wistfulness in a smile,

11 I am the urge in good and moderate desires,

12 I am the gaiety in gladness, the restlessness in life, the refreshment in sleep,

13 yet, though I am in all these, I am not contained in them, and they are in me rather than I am in them,

14 how pitiful are the words of men to depict sublime things!

15 with the souls of men asleep, enwrapped in clouds of delusion, how can I be known to them?

16 I am of the Supreme, the Eternal, of Elohim and from Elohim, yet not Elohim,

17 as heat to fire, as fragrance to flowers, as light to a lamp, so am I to Elohim,

18 I am the power of El operating in matter,

19 I am the first created of creation,

20 I am the Eternal thread upon which all creation is strung,

21 I am the effective thought of Elohim,

22 I am that brought forth by His creating command, wherein all things share life,

23 I am the Adonai of Forms, holding all things together,

24 I am the power giving form,

25 I am the comforting companion of the way,

26 I am also that which gives substance to the hopes and desires of men!

27 think of me therefore in any way you will, I am the companionable one, the comforter,

28 I am the waters of inspiration springing from the Eternal Fount, I am the glory of love shining forth from the Central Light, I am in all things,

29 I am the root of the Tree of Life, the words written in the Book of Adon,

30 I am the guardian of knowledge, the wisdom of the soul,

31 I am the harmoniser of sound, the controller of power, the keeper of matter and the sustainer of shapes,

32 I unroll the scroll of time and record its changes, I am the reader of past and present, the scribe of change, the chooser of chance,

33 I am victory and the struggle for victory, but I am more, I am that which defeats defeat, for I am the victory in defeat,

34 I am the goodness of those who are good, but I am more, for I am the success that arises out of failure, I am the achievement

remaining when all else has gone,

35 I am the sublime veiling secret mysteries,

36 I am the guardian who jealously discloses hidden things!

37 I am the knowledge of the knower,

38 I am the seed within the seed, from which all things spring,

39 I am the bricks of which all things are built, I am more, I am the clay and water within the bricks,

40 I am the motion in all things that move, without me there is no movement,

41 I am the stability in all things stable, without me no thing holds to its shape,

42 I am the craftsman with innumerable shapes, the artist with countless colours,

43 my labours are outside the knowledge of men, my works beyond their sight, my masterpieces will never be seen by mortal eyes!

44 that which abides in breath and yet is other than breath, which breath itself cannot know or influence, which controls it from within itself, that am I,

45 that which is behind the voice, which voice itself cannot know or influence, which controls it from behind itself, that am I,

46 that which is behind the touch, and yet is other than touch, which touch itself cannot know or influence, which manipulates it from behind itself, that am I,

47 yet this you must know: I am not you, nor are you me, though I abide in you, as you abide in me;

48 let wisdom disentangle these feeble words set down through the hands of mortal men!

49 I penetrate Earth with love! I raise up the seed! I am the Breath within the breath of all living things!

50 I am the sweet scent of flowers and the bitter tang of vinegar,

51 I am the differentiating essence in all things.

The Lived Religion - Book 8 - Sayings

Chapter 1

1 Hearken, evil times have befallen the wise and upright,

2 Truth shows her light no more, and deceit walks the land garbed in gay raiment and with a bold front!

3 these times of evil and these days of affliction were foreshadowed by a decline in the goodness of men,

4 by the lust for pleasure among the people and a seeking after things which bring forgetfulness,

5 in carelessness of craftsmanship, in indecision of thought, in disdain for wisdom, and in disregard for the welfare of the land,

6 men think only of earthly things, and therefore Earth becomes a region ruled by wickedness and corruption,

7 therefore, give heed to these sayings, for they are offered for your benefit, they are not things recorded carelessly or without reason!

8 they will enlighten the ignorant, and give all men assurance that they may steer a steady course through life,

9 fill your bellies with them as with cool waters, store them up, as a prudent man stores corn against a time of famine,

10 these instructions will be more honoured and cherished by the Man of Elohim in times of trials and tribulations, than shalom and plenty,

11 my friends, if your desire is the attainment of perfection, beauty, and goodness, along with the knowledge of the ultimate in Truth, then do not be disobedient to The Supreme Elohim!

12 throughout the land, people complain that they have little to live for, but it would be more true to say that they have nothing to die for,

13 they can see no purpose in life, but the truth is they can see no purpose in death!

14 when the light of the Lived Religion is given to the world, it will not be a world ready to welcome it, or even ready to receive it,

15 the world to which it will come will be a sick, disordered world reluctant to take the medicine which will restore it to health,

16 the Lived Religion is not a formula for blind belief,

17 it is not a matter of doctrine alone, and dogmatic belief must not be rigidly imposed,

18 though, loyalty and unity are certainly to be expected from those who follow its light,

19 the Lived Religion is not so much a belief or doctrine, as a way of living, it is the way of life of a company of kindred ruchot headed for the same destination!

20 all sharing the same adventure, with its hazards and excitement, all seeking the best road together,

21 it is a practical religion teaching the doctrine of evolving betterment!

22 it establishes a standard for men to live by, which will make them better men, and permit them to live in shalom and harmony with others,

23 it values the qualities of courage, audacity, fortitude, and steadfastness,

24 it upholds the virtues of modesty, patience, purity, and gentleness,

25 its prime objectives, are to the carrying out of the Divine Design, and the service of mankind,

26 it is a religion lived! and not just believed in,

27 the Lived Religion demands to be expressed in deeds and not in words, in beneficial action and not in blind conformity,

28 it is more interested in bringing out the inward good, than in outward display and pomp,

29 it concerns itself with whatever is necessary for the unfolding of the ruach, and its aim is to spur man upward to Divinity!

30 the Lived Religion believes that man is the instrument of The Divine One, and His deputy on Earth,

31 that man is entrusted with certain responsibilities and duties, which he can shirk only to his cost!

32 whether he succeeds or not, he can blame no one except himself.

Chapter 2

1 Perhaps too much has been said about man's destination, and not enough about the way to get there,

2 a man who travels is better served by information about the road, its turnoffs and landmarks, than about the comfort of his destination,

3 ford the rivers and cross the hills before you concern yourself with the warmth of the lodging when you arrive;

4 most things written here are not for sleeping men, for an infant cannot be entrusted with a firebrand,

5 little purpose is served by talking to a sleeping man, still less to a deaf man, and less still to one who has no desire to hear!

6 so it is that men walk as though in a fog and see things hazily or with distortion,

7 you, my friends, must go out among them and take their hands and be their guides, if they will not follow, they alone suffer,

8 for if you do your best, you can do no more!

9 be vigilant concerning every deed! for the eyes of men are ever upon you,

10 the life you live is not yours alone, you are the image which men will imitate, and you are before every eye, selah;

11 the blowing wind will open its ear at your windows and spread wide its report, the flowing waters beside your door will carry what they behold through the land!

12 the apathetic man becomes deluded under the influence of his

own ideas and imagination, he readily accepts teachings requiring no thought or effort,

13 if ever a teacher comes along who says, "Surrender your will and reason to me, and I will assure you of Life Everlasting!" that teacher will be unable to count his followers;

14 there are things buried in the future with which it is unprofitable to deal, so what is said in the Scripture must suffice,

15 better by far to deal with the problems of today, though even these are less important than learning the nature of Elohim;

16 to act as men do when worshipping is to belittle The Supreme Elohim,

17 how can One so great be worshipped and served by fires and candles? by mumbled words falling thoughtlessly on unhearing ears? by ornaments and incense?

18 these things may serve a purpose in aiding man's awakening, but it is hypocritical to say they are necessary to The Supreme Elohim, and blasphemy to say He requires them from man!

19 the Supreme Elohim rises above the worship of men, and says, "If such things please man, then let the offerer become the recipient,

20 the truly enlightened worship Me by a compliment,

21 in trying to match their purity and goodness with My reflection of these qualities coming down from On High,

22 this is true worship: The ennobling of the lesser self,

23 goodness in thought, word, and deed,

24 the subjection of material urges,

25 a constant disciplining of the body,

26 and an unwavering devotion to the cause of mankind! which is the Cause of Adonai!

27 these please Me, provided they are not clouded with hypocrisy."

Chapter 3

1 This is the secret of life: Man lives in Elohim and Elohim lives in man! this answers all questions,

2 a child is born knowing all Adon intended it to know, the rest, it must discover for itself;

3 man worships, not to make Elohim greater, for this he cannot do, but to make himself greater,

4 nothing man can do can add to what He already has;

5 man does not live to increase My glory, this cannot be done!

6 he who worships with empty rituals wastes his time, and displays the shallowness of his thought,

7 men conceive Me as a Being having greatly magnified human qualities, as a Kinglike Being greater than any king, thus, man falls into error,

8 if a man would know Heaven, he must first know Earth, man cannot understand Heaven until he understands Earth,

9 he cannot understand Me until he understands himself, and he cannot know love unless he has been loveless;

10 Elohim is unknown, but not unknowable, He is unseen, but not unseeable,

11 Elohim is unheard, but not unhearable, He is not understood, but He is understandable,

12 the best way to know and understand anything is to study its properties, and this applies to The Supreme Elohim, so therefore consider: What is beauty? what is goodness? what is perfection?

13 can any man think long on the wonder of creation and the complexity of created things, and declare truthfully that he believes they came into being of their own accord?

14 can he look at the awesome beauty of the spinning heavens, now so old and yet so full of vitality, with never a sign of declining powers, and say there is no Motivator behind it?

15 can he look at the life-giving light of day and the growth-controlling light of the night, at the teeming Earth and stars, and honestly believe that all this is a matter of pure chance?

16 could all this vast and splendidly run universe have created itself? it could, if a tapestry can weave itself, or a statue chisel itself out from the rock.

Chapter 4

1 There are men without merit themselves, they appeal to the deeds of their forefathers for credit,

2 what good is it to the blind man that his father could see? what benefit to the illiterate that his father could write?

3 is it not more to his discredit that he is what he is?

4 he who walks in the shadow of his father's reputation has none of his own,

5 he who establishes his reputation upon that of another erects a building without foundation,

6 even the ass of Pharaoh is still an ass,

7 a worthless man does worthless things, his death removes an encumbrance from the Earth!

8 a wise man is one who bathes in the waters of wisdom, a fool is one who wallows in the filth of folly;

9 the well of wisdom is not a public place from which anyone may draw without discrimination,

10 its entrance is barred to he of the loud mouth, but opens to receive the calm and silent one,

11 though, where today are the men of quiet manner and calm bearing?

12 no wise words or well-phrased writings are needed to inform men that the light of the sun exceeds that of the moon,

13 or that he who has toiled through the heat of the day will not lie on a bed of sleeplessness,

14 things experienced by a few, that are unknown to the many, have to be explained, such are ruach-ual things,

15 but where today are those who have known and experienced them? who can explain them to others?

16 words are unimportant to prayer, for good and fine words alone are not edifying to Elohim,

17 He hears that which is spoken from the heart and reads that which is written in the soul, therefore, those who are answered are few,

18 those who are not, because of their own inadequacy, say, "Where is Elohim? He hears me not!"

19 the souls of men, swathed in flesh and wrapped in passions, cannot easily commune with Elohim,

20 if one write so that none can read it, is the reader or the writer at fault if it cannot deliver its message?

21 successful prayer needs much conditioning of the soul, it requires a lot of preliminary preparation, and is, therefore, rare!

22 men say, "Prayer is futility," and to such as they, so it is!

23 the ingredients of prayer are humility, sincerity, surrender of desire, acknowledgement of inadequacy, and a wholehearted offering of self!

24 it is the opening of a door to admit a wonderful power into the chambers of the soul!

25 prayer, as it should be, is followed by a profound shalom, a ruach-ual uplifting, and a feeling of inner quietude,

26 as though a cool, clean breeze sweeps into the ruach,

strengthening and reviving it, so that clear-thinking follows naturally!

27 when at prayer, listen to the voice of your ruach, for it may be interpreting the Words of Abba Adonai,

28 prayer renders the soul articulate!

29 the length of prayer is unimportant, but the depth and range of prayer matters above all else,

30 prayer is a state of harmony embracing heart and ruach, it is not a rite,

31 prayer is the communication of the soul of man with the Soul of Elohim,

32 it is the effective means whereby the great well of Ruach-ual power and inspiration is tapped!

33 above all, it is not a babble of words.

Chapter 5

1 Torot are made by man, and the same torot are changed by other men, while yet more live in defiance,

2 but no man on Earth truly knows what is right and what is wrong, the Torot of Life can be discovered only in the Inspired Writings!

3 the time is not far distant when men should no longer think in terms of being good or wicked, rich or poor, sick or healthy, but in terms of being ruach-ual or material,

4 O man, who is both beast and elohim, see yourself for what you truly are! be reasonable and see Truth!

5 every thinking man must surely realise now that there is something more to life than happiness, wealth, and luxury?

6 that life must be more than an idle drifting? that there must be more than walking around seeking enjoyment?

7 in his daily life and in all he does, each man should conduct himself as though intending to be a living example to others,

8 he should act as though dedication to service is the greatest cause any man can serve, and invite others to join him,

9 he should be a leader showing the way, and a guide indicating the path others should follow, though the journey each must walk alone;

10 unless they would be put out by the mockers, carriers of the light must possess more than a dim smoky glimmer;

11 the goal of life is upstream, not downstream, man must struggle against the current, not drift with the flow;

12 among men, some are born to rule and some to obey,

13 if then you cannot rule, learn to obey,

14 if you cannot obey, make yourself a better man, that you may be raised up to rule;

15 that which man does to benefit man is good, one lifting hand is worth ten wagging tongues;

16 though it is folly to sit irresolutely at the crossroads, is it wiser

to press forward along the wrong road?

17 those who seek to assert their individuality at the expense of others are a menace not to be tolerated!

18 everyone is to be granted the greatest possible freedom, up to, but not beyond the point where it infringes upon the freedom, rights, or contentment of others,

19 it is impossible to give complete freedom to any man, and no man is worthy of it!

20 the only man entitled to be free is the one who governs himself strictly and wisely,

21 the free man is his own governor, and his rule is more rigorous than that of a despot,

22 a man is unworthy of freedom unless he also recognises the rights of others to the same freedom,

23 every nation moves either towards freedom or towards servility, for none can remain suspended between the two,

24 it is free men, if they are weak, who are the greatest enemies of freedom!

Chapter 6

1 Great events do not make either heroes or weaklings, they just unveil them to the eyes of other men;

2 if you pray out of habit or give generously for praise, or if you do good for the sake of acclaim, then you are a hypocrite,

3 the hypocrite, the liar, and the deceiver are brothers, and all distort their souls, Truth can fall from their lips, but it is usually in the form of bait;

4 for the wrongdoer and he who walks in wickedness, the passing years plant more wrinkles and scars on the face of the soul, than on the face of the body;

5 speak not until you have full understanding of a matter, and can explain it even to he who knows more;

6 in matters close to your heart, never fear that you will be lost for words,

7 for if the heart be wrung the mouth will open in eloquence, but be wise, even a dog makes a noise when kicked;

8 men bear the burden of their body with unintended sadness,

9 they are like a man living in an empty tomb, who shrinks from the bright sunlight outside,

10 the longer he hesitates, the whiter and weaker his body becomes;

11 it is not so important to give to the poor man, as to remove the cause of his poverty,

12 to help the weak is good, but of lesser importance than to attack their oppressor!

13 my friends, the world need not be a place overrun with evil, if men could only cleanse the garments of their minds, it could be a place of unceasing joy!

14 look for the man of merit and see that he does not go

unrewarded,

15 encourage the craftsman and promote useful works,

16 let your wealth serve all men and not be dissipated in selfish indulgences!

17 seek out the promoters of poverty and distress, and cast your riches in the balances against them,

18 do not expect life to reward you or even grant you shalom or pleasure,

19 the powerful and strong will be your enemies, and even those you serve will betray you,

20 you will not be acclaimed and may even be derided as a fool, only, your soul will remain steadfast beside you!

21 if you asked for one rule to guide you safely, I would say to ignore the authoritative voice of the body, and listen to the quiet whispers of the soul.

Chapter 7

1 A rich man is not wicked because of his riches, for this of itself neither makes a man wicked nor makes him good,

2 it is the manner whereby he deals with his riches that determines a man's status,

3 there is little advantage in the mere possession of riches, the advantage is gained in knowing how to use them,

4 the riches which exceed your modest requirements are

superfluous to your welfare, it is by your dealings with the surplus that you will be judged!

5 let not your generosity be hampered by the riches you have, rejoice in their possession, for if used for good, your pleasure is without blame,

6 but he who stores up riches beyond his needs and puts them to no good use swathes his soul in the wrappings of death!

7 so wait not until men come seeking your compassion, find them first! and assist them without desiring praise or benefit,

8 let your ear be ever alert for the cry of the needy! and your arm be ever ready to aid the unprotected!

9 let the sorrow of innocent suffering never go unheeded!

10 pour forth succour to those who can find no other to aid them,

11 when the widow and orphan beseech your aid with eyes of suffering, open the gates of compassion within your heart,

12 for he who turns from the rags of the destitute and ignores the pale cheek of the hungry smites his soul with paralysing blows,

13 is it a matter for wonder that it becomes dead and insensitive? unfeeling and unresponsive?

14 if for no other reason, have compassion on others for your own sake! for it moulds your greater form in a Glory Everlasting!

15 while even one man groans in misery in the habitations of poverty, or there remains one grey head bowed with distress to plead for aid,

16 how can you go your way unmoved by compassion? dissipating your time and substance in unprofitable enjoyments?

17 you who indulge in vain pleasures, unfeelingly, while others want and suffer, will some day eat your own heart out in the dark barrenness within the gloomy depths, haunted by bitterness and regret!

18 of what good are gold and silver when an abundance causes so much wickedness?

19 the metals the Great Adon placed in the bosom of Earth to serve man have become his master,

20 blame not the metals, for they of themselves are neutral,

21 but behold, are they not found in abundant quantities among the worst types of men?

22 are they not held in greatest esteem by the weakling? who thinks they provide a substitute for the strength he lacks?

23 if you have become great, having once been lowly or if having been destitute, have now acquired possessions, forget not what has happened to you in the days that are passed,

24 place not your whole trust, nor build your hopes on the things which have, after all, but come as a gift from Elohim,

25 you would not be superior to any other man if what had happened to you, had happened to them,

26 is it by your own manliness and goodness that you have risen?

27 if rich, become not puffed up because of your possessions, or if poor, be not downhearted, for Elohim in His wisdom has

presented you this test!

28 the poor man says, "O, that I had riches and could be free from worry and care!"

29 the rich man says, "O, that I could cast aside my responsibilities and live in shalom!"

30 if you be numbered among the poor, take comfort, for you have many causes for thankfulness:

31 Can you not sit at your table with a quiet mind? undisturbed by the clacking tongues of flatterers and hypocrites?

32 do the demands of needy men disturb your shalom?

33 does the morsel you eat not taste wholesome? in the stomach of the rich, it would sit as a stone,

34 possessions and position attract friends as honey attracts bees, but it is adversity which winnows them,

35 riches do not bring shalom to the soul, and the greatest treasure of all is a contented heart,

36 men test gold for its value, and gold tests men for their hearts!

37 a piece of arable land fenced about, a plot of meadow, a grove of sycamore trees, a faithful wife and many sons, what more can a man desire?

Chapter 8

1 When you give, consider well the deed, is it really you who gives?

2 is it not more true to say it is life giving to life? a transfer from one guardian of life to another?

3 what are you but the instrument? the witness? the agent of the transaction?

4 you are the debtor of life, for has it not given you all you have?

5 if there be among men one who has received nothing from life, then let him be the one who refuses to give!

6 the good giver gives and thereafter does not remember the gift, the receiver, if he be worthy, never forgets it;

7 none is worse than the mean man who has riches and estate, for he rides heavily on the backs of his servants and waxes fat on the sweat of their brows,

8 he is without compassion or feeling, and the ruin of his brother brings him no sorrow,

9 for the increase in his riches, the mean man secretly rejoices in the death of his father, and he, being also hypocritical, will be loudest in lamentation;

10 the mean man and the braggart may seem incompatible, but man is a many-sided creature,

11 the mean and miserly heart and the most boastful tongue so often share the same body;

12 to gather riches for their own sake corrupts the soul, but to deal with them to the benefit of others beautifies it!

13 see the face of the miser and imagine the dark horror it dimly

reflects, and behold the face of the benevolent man, does it not mirror the radiance within?

14 be faithful to the trust which your master reposes in you, that you may be more trusted and become greater,

15 the time and labour for which he pays belong to him, and if dealt with indifferently, you rob him!

16 never injure the arm that protects you or undermine the supports for the roof that provides shelter;

17 he serves best who serves silently, the trusted servant is he who keeps his tongue in check;

18 a wagging tongue has its roots in a quaking heart;

19 go quietly about your task, the reward is your own self-respect, knowing that it is well done;

20 the peasant steals handful by handful, and the prince steals load by load, and it is better to have clean hands than full ones!

21 the wrongdoer becomes a slave to his own wickedness, therefore, do that which is right, and your ruach shall remain free!

Chapter 9

1 The busiest tongue has the least cause to wag, what does it seek to cover up?

2 govern yourself and you can rule the land, but the best way to succeed is to follow the advice you give others;

3 most men can beat adversity well enough, but if you really want

to test a man, give him power;

4 if undertaking a great enterprise, ensure the support of a trustworthy friend, for nothing can be done unaided,

5 even when burning a field of stubble, the aid of the wind is necessary;

6 the price of success is continued diligence and effort!

7 for though gold may be melted completely, let the fire grow cold, and it hardens again;

8 seek not to dwell within the shadow of a man because of his estate or because he has titles, better men may be lacking these,

9 do you judge the ass by its bridle?

10 is not your neighbour worthy of your consideration? is he not your partner in Earth? your brother in Elohim?

11 no man is worthy to judge the failings of another, unless he too has experienced their temptations,

12 it is easy enough to see the failings of another, this any man can do, and even easier to sit in judgment on them, but it takes a thoughtful man to see the failings of his own;

13 never go about among men with a sad face,

14 men care not for the countenance of gloom, but that which is pleasant is easy to remember,

15 it is easy for a man to appear great when he is great, but difficult for a man to appear pleasant and agreeable when he is neither,

16 though if your talents are such that you cannot appear great in the sight of others, you can approach greatness, by being pleasant and agreeable,

17 the sad face, reflecting a gloomy heart, will deaden even the joyfulness of youth.

Chapter 10

1 The greatest attribute of man, and the most dangerous and discomforting gift of El, is freewill! most men use it unwisely, yet it is the golden promise of elohim-hood!

2 be cautious at all times, two arrows in the quiver are better than one, and three better still;

3 at all times leaven your deeds with caution and measure them with prudence as a guide,

4 for as the whirlwind raises the sweeping sandstorm that overwhelms the works of men,

5 so does the irresponsible voice of the multitude overwhelm reason in those who heed it without judgment;

6 guests always bring pleasure of some kind, if not in their arrival, then with their departure;

7 if one comes with a request, never say, "Come again tomorrow and I will give," when it is in your power to grant it today;

8 consider your family and friends, what they are like, for they are clear pools wherein you see yourself reflected,

9 a man has the wife, family, and friends he deserves!

10 is your dwelling a haven of joy in a sea of sorrow? is it the treasure house of sympathy and understanding?

11 or do you reside in a place harbouring nought but luxury and comfort? where the stifling air is befouled with the unwholesome lust for ease?

12 comfort can always be invited in as a guest, but beware lest it stay to rule the household,

13 it is easier to be the slave of luxury than the master;

14 the virgin soil is yours to cultivate as you will, it is fertile and responsive! let it not want for care, for if it be unhusbanded, it will remain barren and unproductive,

15 the good pasture that is neglected produces weeds in abundance, and who is blamed, the pasture? or the husbandman?

16 the seed which you sow will produce a crop to be reaped in the fullness of time!

17 the weeds you neglect to pull up will multiply and pollute the harvest!

18 brothers, a harvest of gladness and pride can be yours! as according to your sowing and attention, so shall you reap!

19 to know the Plan of the Most High Adonai is not enough, the Scriptures are not given to be just known, but to be lived!

20 you may have knowledge of the words written, but do you also live them in your heart?

21 after listening to the words of a wise master, one said, "You are unbending in your teachings, is it not wise to follow the path of moderation?"

22 the master answered, "I am not interested in moderate faith or moderate goodness, moderate honesty or moderate virtue,

23 there can be no moderation in things of vital importance! the moderate man is not for me,

24 would you eat a moderately fresh egg? or want to live in a house that keeps out most of the wind and rain? would you be satisfied with most of your wages?

25 a standard of moderate morality is no standard at all,"

26 another stranger then accosted the master, and said, "The doctrine you teach is sound, but I don't like your methods,"

27 the master answered, "Is that so? well, actually, I am not too satisfied with them myself,

28 tell me, how do you inspire men to live in harmony among themselves?"

29 the stranger paused and said, "I don't,"

30 replied the master, "Then, I prefer the way I do it, to the way you don't!"

31 let this written wisdom be the straight edge to show how much you deviate from the true, use it to align yourself, to eliminate the crookedness!

32 not the least purpose of these writings is to reveal your weaknesses, to remind you that your body is but dust,

33 and to stimulate your ruach with the joyous knowledge of the glories awaiting your awakened soul!

Chapter 11

1 Seek always after shalom and quietude, and find friends among the silent ones,

2 the man who fears to be alone with himself in silence or solitude will never discover the secrets of the soul,

3 some men go into the wilderness to commune with their soul in silence, and there do they receive a reply;

4 discretion and caution are not akin to cowardice, even the ants scout before moving in force;

5 it is wise to cross the field before you abuse the bull and learn to swim before you rock the boat;

6 the basic motive behind a righteous and good life, is not the quest for happiness,

7 righteousness, goodness, and morality are other words meaning self-discipline, duty, obligation, and service,

8 these form a foundation upon which a proper way of life can be built,

9 and within the framework of this foundation, the quest for happiness is certainly not restricted, indeed, not only is it encouraged, but also earnestly urged!

10 as far as man is concerned, the purpose of his life is the

development and preparation of his soul for something greater,

11 this cannot be undertaken in a half-hearted manner or at specific times, it is a process continuing every minute of the day!

12 every test confronting man here is purposeful and necessary, even though its reason and end may be obscure;

13 forget what has been done and cannot be altered, and do not be concerned about things which may never happen,

14 devote your attention to the present, and gain the most from life!

15 arise early in the morning and greet the day eagerly, for the sluggard and lie-a-bed are already partially dead;

16 if you have anything of value, keep it away from an envious man;

17 eat and drink in moderation, taking sufficient for the wellbeing of the body without overloading it;

18 be proud but not haughty, straight-talking but not insulting,

19 be bold but not aggressive, patient but not servile,

20 bear in mind that it is better for a man to be numbered among the insulted than among the insulters, among the slandered and not among the slanderers;

21 if visited by affliction or sorrow, a man should not bewail his lot, for these should be the means of drawing him closer into the embrace of Divinity!

22 they are meant to strengthen his ruach and develop his ruach-

uality,

23 no man has any right to expect an untroubled life,

24 and one who has passed half a year without trouble or affliction has already received ample reward for living, and should not feel entitled for more,

25 while man walks Earth, sorrow ever dogs his footsteps, it will come close enough unbidden, therefore encourage it not with your own ill judgment!

26 sorrow is the purging agent of the ruach, and suffering the flux merging man with Divinity, they also help to distinguish purelove from mocklove,

27 for purelove is the unquenchable fire which the waters of tribulation cannot put out!

28 the good and the wicked are tested, and no one is exempt,

29 the difference is that the righteous man uses the tests to benefit himself,

30 while the unrighteous turns them against himself, and Elohim, to destroy his own soul!

31 no man should be overwhelmed by the troubles and tribulations which come upon him,

32 they are intended to be utilised for the benefit of his soul and the strengthening of his ruach, and bearing this in mind, he should be better able to endure them,

33 in the greater scheme of things, the times of affliction and adversity are not to be feared so much, for then men incline

towards ruach-ual things,

34 it is in times of prosperity, when they acquire wealth and become conceited and self-centred, that the danger lies,

35 for then they twist the commanding words and austere meanings of the Kodesh Books! and pervert them to console their own consciences!

36 therefore in times of prosperity and contentment, a man must be more careful in the interpretation of the Kodesh Books than he would be when he only turned to them for strength and consolation.

Chapter 12

1 Never try to appease a man in the hour of his anger, leave him to be consumed in his own fire!

2 when two persons quarrel in anger, both are always in the wrong,

3 before you vent your anger on a man who has offended you, selah, and try to discover some goodness in him, which you lack,

4 it is not required that a person never get angry or become stirred up inside, for sometimes circumstances demand the response of righteous anger!

5 therefore, be one slow to anger and with complete mastery over the temper, rather than one without the ability to be stirred to anger,

6 do not be too sweet unless you want to be eaten;

7 few are those who recognise their own defects, and fewer still those who honestly acknowledge them,

8 even less in number are those who earnestly strive to overcome them, though, this is an essential part of life's purpose,

9 most men are hypocrites and self-deceivers!

10 one of the greatest defects of character is sheer indifference and lack of interest in anything greater,

11 a man can gain wisdom and enlightenment only when he has laboured at reading and diligently studying the Kodesh Books!

12 casual thinking about Higher things and reading for amusement or pleasure produce no beneficial effect, and serve no useful purpose;

13 the man of sound character bestirs himself in the cause of good, and diligently studies the Kodesh Books to know what is required of him,

14 he accepts with good grace the tasks imposed upon him and does not shirk his duties and obligations,

15 he does not try to interpret the teachings of the Kodesh Books in such a way that things are made easier for him,

16 he does not treat their command lightly, neither does he shun the service they require from him,

17 he knows that no matter how hard he strives, they can still lead him on towards greater perfection!

18 no man is asked to be perfect, he is asked only to strive towards perfection with all his heart and strength!

19 avoid those whose natures are shallow or superficial, even though they be attractive and pleasant,

20 shallow streams sparkle most, and weakest waters make the most pleasant sound.

Chapter 13

1 There are many, whose understanding of friendship is mere companionship, and they neither seek nor know anything deeper,

2 such people should not be cultivated beyond acquaintanceship;

3 no man really knows another until he has seen him exposed to danger and loss,

4 even then, he cannot know him fully until he has seen him when tested by prosperity and success;

5 man is to make the most of conditions as he finds them and get all the happiness he can from life, within the framework laid down in the Kodesh Books,

6 earthly conditions are not to be accepted passively!

7 for every man has a duty to make some improvement, however slight, upon the earthly state of things,

8 not only must he make the best of earthly conditions, but he must also improve them, so that more happiness may be gained!

9 though this may appear to serve only an earthly end, it is not entirely the case, for in the effort lies the ruach-ual development;

10 the amount of ruach-ual experience and enlightenment permitted any man is just sufficient not to upset the balance of his life or nullify his earthly existence,

11 this is a fact which should be clearly understood by those ignorant persons who rail against the lack of Divine intervention or guidance, selah;

12 followers of the Lived Religion enjoy a balanced, harmonious life! and a life well and profitably lived!

13 it is a life of many contrasts and experiences, with a steady advance towards ruach-uality,

14 all earthly goals are elusive, and their attainment may not bring the pleasure and happiness anticipated,

15 there is only one goal towards which everyone can advance with certainty and assurance, and that is the goal of an awakened soul!

16 the very things which defeat earthly ends and render them impossible to accomplish, are, if viewed in the proper perspective, aids towards the achievement of ruach-uality,

17 out of earthly failure and frustration can come ruach-ual accomplishment and gain, if you can understand this, the good life is yours!

18 conscience is the best guide and experience the best teacher,

19 nature is the best book and life the highest form of schooling, death is the great graduation day!

20 the purpose of learning is to know the good from the bad, the beneficial from the harmful,

21 the good and beneficial should not be scorned, whoever dispenses them,

22 would you take poison even if offered by your best friend? or refuse dressing for a wound because it is given by an enemy?

23 because there are many false prophets, the words of a true prophet do not lose their value! no man has ever sought to counterfeit a valueless thing,

24 the vine is judged by the drink it produces and not by its leaves and appearance, it is the end product that matters!

25 the outward vestments of a religion are unimportant, for gaudy ones may hide a festering ruach, while unimposing garments may clothe a healthy one,

26 disregard the bottle and give your attention to its contents;

27 I do not expect man to achieve perfection here on Earth, but only to seek it,

28 what is expected of man is a sincere and honest effort, without any hypocritical or deceptive reservations!

29 My Divine Design requires that man make a conscious choice of right, under the constant pressure of temptation to do otherwise, this also leaves man free to choose wrong,

30 man chooses wrong instead of right for just two reasons: Either it is the easy path of least resistance, or it is the most alluring.

Chapter 14

1 On Earth, the body is equally as important as the soul, keep it clean and in good health, that it may fittingly render such service as the soul requires,

2 the nearest approach that can be made to complete bliss on Earth is to enjoy the blessing of good health!

3 remember that the call of the food table exceeds the needs of the body,

4 the man who overeats is worse than the beast who knows no better,

5 eat only when hungry and drink only when thirsty,

6 and consume food slowly and with content, for a restless stomach robs it of taste and goodness;

7 to overeat is as harmful as to starve,

8 eat to fill a third part of the stomach, drink to fill a third part, and leave the rest empty;

9 to fast is not an empty deed and is healthful for both ruach and body! it teaches discipline and self-control, as well as moderation and frugality,

10 gluttony is a disgrace to manhood, for as a man grows in girth, he declines in vigour, one thing replaces another,

11 he who eats little is zestful, while he who gorges himself is sluggish,

12 he whose greatest interest lies in satisfying the demands of the stomach is a reproach to manhood, for he is dominated by his

appetite,

13 the stomach always cries for more than it requires!

14 sufficient food maintains health, overmuch destroys it,

15 beer drunk in moderation does no harm, and wine in small quantities can bring contentment and pleasure!

16 be kind to your body, which is the vehicle of your pilgrimage and the chariot of your conquest, keep it in health and strength, that you may enjoy life with vigour!

17 it was not meant that the body should be neglected, and in fact, the Torah ordains that recompense be made for a neglected body!

18 a body made weak by dissipation and gross from fat living is an abomination unto the Adon of Life!

19 if the head is unclean, it will lead to blindness,

20 if the garments worn are unclean, it will lead to madness,

21 if the body is unclean, it will lead to sores and sickness;

22 do not overeat or oversleep, for body rust is not an unreal thing.

Chapter 15

1 Joy and contentment come from something a man has within himself, not from things without,

2 solitude is a torment to the uneasy heart, but balm to the contented one;

3 the well done task that encompasses your day brings healthy sleep in its train,

4 do not weary yourself concerning the affairs of the day, nor be over anxious about your household and estate,

5 things happen, disaster or power come according to the dispensations of Elohim!

6 follow your inclinations, and if your plans go awry, continue in shalom,

7 do your best, and be content that you can do no more!

8 let your heart be quiet within your body, and your body will not be unhealthy,

9 the body is the guest chamber of the soul! let the soul not abide in squalor;

10 the rule is moderation in all things,

11 turn from unmanly ways, follow the path of cleanliness, and avoid the indulgences of soft living and iniquity!

12 follow these sayings and sleep soundly! spend your waking hours in shalom!

13 do not accustom yourself to lying in bed while the dawn is breaking in beauty, for no man is truly wholesome unless he has knowledge of the dawn,

14 the cup of gladness may be sipped by man, but to drain it is too much for the constitution of mortals,

15 enjoy life! take whatever it gives with high-ruchot,

16 when it bestows contentment, be contented,

17 when life presents the test, rise above it! and when disaster strikes, meet it like a man!

18 contentment is a worthy goal of life, but first the race has to be run,

19 none can receive the crown of the victor until the course is finished and he takes his place among the competitors in the Halls of Eternity!

20 therefore, be content if your burdens are bearable and your sorrows counterbalanced by your joys,

21 remember that pleasure is the companion, not the guide, of your journey,

22 contentment is a state of mind, not an end, but he who is content with anything deserves nothing!

23 the days that are past have gone forever, and those that sleep in the womb of the future may not be beheld by you in your present state of being,

24 therefore it is well to concern yourself wholly with the present, forgetting the past, and not expecting too much from the future,

25 live today fully! sigh not for tomorrow, for it will come! regret not yesterday, for it is gone!

26 from whence does sadness come? not from external circumstances, but from a worm within the heart,

27 it can have no existence, but for the sustenance it saps from your own feebleness of ruach,

28 sorrow there will always be, for the Torah decrees that it is essential for the tempering of the ruach,

29 but sorrow is another adversary to conquer and cast out! it is not something to be accepted with resignation,

30 the greatest benefit comes from rising above it, therefore let your face shine with cheerfulness!

31 for a cheerful countenance will bring brightness even into the lives of the afflicted, and gladness even to the most distressed.

Chapter 16

1 It is decreed, by the nature of things, that womankind should fall into two groups,

2 and each woman is to be dealt with according to the category in which she has placed herself:

3 These are the two categories of womankind: Wives or potential wives, and women of pleasure;

4 the first of these are the intended mates of men, their companions and comforters, the mothers of their children, and the keepers of their hearths!

5 the others become their companions in carnal pleasure, they dally with them, then cast them aside, as they pass on to the embrace of other uncaring men!

6 each woman decides which category she will join, and that is

her chosen path;

7 never confuse the two kinds of women, lest you eat out your heart in sorrow and regret!

8 be considerate, for the husband without consideration prepares his own betrayal;

9 if you commit adultery, then prepare to flee, for men will arise against you,

10 for if they revile not the adulterer, nor raise their arms against him, all men must look to their own wives,

11 if men fail to punish the adulterer, then they encourage the seduction of their own women,

12 in the land of weaklings, the adulterer hunts freely, for who will oppose him?

13 is it not written, "That which is not punished is condoned?"

14 when a woman whose husband is absent displays her beauty and encourages your visit,

15 when she arranges that there be no witnesses and prepares her net for you,

16 then is the hour of your manhood's trial! depart from her house, for it is a place of evil!

17 if you are unfortunate and unwise enough to love the wife of another man, then degrade not that love by expressing it in dark corners like a cur,

18 go to the husband, like a man, and let events happen as they

will;

19 he who defiles the home of another cannot be justly wrathful if his own is defiled;

20 the beauty of womanhood was ordained to inspire man, and of all things it is his greatest incentive to achievement!

21 therefore a woman's secrets are not to be lightly attained,

22 the evil of the harlot is that she counters the inspiration of womanhood, her wickedness is her cheapness!

23 the pleasures of a harlot are of the body and exist only for the moment, to pass into nothingness like a dream,

24 therefore be wise in your dealings with women, and to be wise is to be prudent and strong!

25 reject that which is easily given, for it will be shared with many men,

26 seek only that which is desirable in its near unattainability, for it will be yours alone,

27 no man is more generous than he who marries a common woman, for he shares her with the multitude!

28 when you find a good woman, cherish her as your greatest treasure! let your kindness and consideration take possession of her heart,

29 she is the mistress in your home, so treat her with respect, that the children shall obey her, and the stranger treat her with diffidence,

30 for if a man treats not his wife with respect, can he take offence when others, observing this, treat her likewise?

31 home is not where the body rests, but where the heart resides, and also where a man receives the most care for the least thanks,

32 a good residence is built on a rock, a good home is established around a good woman!

33 a man loves his mother and his father, his sisters and his brothers, all his life, yet they are not of his choosing,

34 how much more likely should it be that he would love his wife, whom he himself chooses? or is man's judgment less wise than that of fate?

35 nothing will ever bring you greater pleasure and joy than a good wife, or more sorrow than a bad one,

36 yet of all things he does bearing on his life and future, a man generally uses the least wisdom when choosing a wife.

The Lived Religion - Book 9 - The Prophet

Chapter 1

1 I am a prophet of the written Word, a man with many Books of Kodesh Wisdom, who comes to you in the Name of The Supreme Elohim!

2 I bear proof of my mission for all to see; I was charged by an Instructing Ruach with the burden of a prophet, it saying,

3 "Go forth into the highways and byways of the land, bearing the scars of one seared by nearness to the Flame of Truth!

4 be not a man of pleasure, nor a son of wickedness, have no love of comfort and the flattery of fine clothes,

5 deceive no woman for fleeting satisfaction, nor be deceived by worldly shadows,

6 here, you have seen with the eyes of man and know the nature of earthly things, are they not shadowy forms without substance, in which no trust can be placed?

7 all earthly things pass away, the loveliness of flowers withers and fades as the beauty of a woman's face slips away with the passing years,"

8 the voice of an Instructing Ruach continued,

9 "Go forth, shaker of those who slumber in ruach, go, stir up the minds of men, crying,

10 'Awake! bestir your true self within the flesh which is doomed to decay, cast off the fetters of worldliness and uncover the eyes

of the soul!'

11 go, gather the sincere seekers and reveal to them a little light, guide them through the bewitching land of earthly illusion, so they leave it to enter the light of Truth, and not the darkness of death!"

12 hearing these things, I said, "Who am I to be a prophet to men?"

13 the voice of an Instructing Ruach came to me, "Be comforted, my son, by the knowledge of Truth,

14 go, submit yourself to life, the harsh taskmaster and gentle saviour, your own good works are not sufficient to pay the cost of entry into the Place of Light!"

15 I asked in sorrow, "Am I then a man of small righteous credit?" and the voice of the Instructing Ruach replied,

16 "Where is the righteous man who is blameless? all men are prone to error, for it is the father of courage and resolution!

17 you have been found reliable in testing, and fit for the covenant of prophesy,"

18 I speak with the words of the Ruach of Elohim, and I am its mouthpiece to men on Earth!

19 I will become an attraction for tribulation, be overwhelmed with troubles, rejected and mocked,

20 "You will be a physician dispensing a bitter draught, the message you bear will not strike men's ears like a charming love song, the words will not fall pleasantly like notes from a well-played harp;

21 pleasant things are fleeting and stir the hearts of men for only a brief moment, entertaining things are soon forgotten, and amusing things leave no mark;

22 your tongue will be a sting and your mouth a fiery furnace,

23 men will hear your words, but they will not penetrate to many hearts,

24 your hearers will say, 'We are much moved and our hearts charged with righteousness,' but these are words of wind, and their hearts will still follow the corrupting inclinations of their desires!"

25 from that day, I came to love life as never before! from that day, I was a lover of Truth!

26 now I no longer have any trust in the world, I am no longer deceived by its ways, I know the world and the works of men, and I know myself,

27 I sought for my soul, and I found myself,

28 I found Truth, and she stands higher than all the world!

29 I learned the secret of the serpent with its tail in its mouth, I saw the workings of the spawn of evil and the fungus of corruption,

30 I gazed upon the Dark Ones, and when they saw me they became vicious, they sought to attach themselves to me, but I was strengthened against them and came forth uncontaminated!

31 when the implications of my fate awoke knowledge in my heart, I wept for my wife, for my children, for would they not

become fatherless?

32 who would harness the oxen and scatter the seed over the soil? who would tend the sheep and stand guard? who would protect from intruders?

33 the Voice said, "The path of the prophet is beset with sorrow,

34 your house is destined to become desolate,

35 your lands shall be abandoned to wild creatures, and many years shall pass before they are resown,"

36 then I said, "Let my wife be spared, and the children of my body? for they will be comforters to me along the way, and strengthen my heart in service,"

37 the voice of the Instructing Ruach replied,

38 "Were these things within my power to grant, gladly would it be done, but you have been chosen as a prophet, and the way is hard and lonely,

39 in the years ahead, your family will be mankind, and I will be your companion;

40 the road is long, and its end rests in Eternity,

41 fear lurks by the wayside, doubt haunts the forest to be traversed, and worldly temptations will be like wolves at your heels,

42 but, you can look forward to the joy of reunion at the destination!

43 and though the way is hard, the journey is not in vain."

Chapter 2

1 Behold, I am the prophet of the day, now hear my voice! there is a Torah of Compensation: Good always leads to good, and bad always to bad,

2 know that whatever the demands made upon you, they are always within reason;

3 to you who defraud the poor and oppress the weak and defenceless, I tell you, your Day is coming!

4 you who make justice a bitter draught or two-pronged weapon, or who twist the torah of the land to suit selfish ends, you shall not escape the remorseless Divine Justice!

5 you who hate those who expose your evil ways and drag dark deeds out into the light of day, you scorners of honest men, you bribers and acceptors of bribes,

6 have a pleasant hour! for a grimmer Day will dawn!

7 you who harvest in fields you have not ploughed, who snatch a few pennies from the poverty stricken,

8 you who connive with the forces of ignorance, who are self-deceivers thinking yourselves learned,

9 you who walk in the comforting security of El-bestowed riches, unheeding of your duty, enjoy your hour! the Reckoning awaits!

10 you who are self-satisfied, priest-deluded, going about like blind men led by the blind, who dwell under a cloud of shamelessness, gaining riches and power by the ignorance and

weakness of others,

11 you who say, "By our own strength have we accomplished our own ends," rejoice while you may! that Day will come, and what will you have then?

12 the inheritance of Eternity is for the upright and frugal, but the wicked and wasters shall be shut out from the places of contentment and shalom,

13 hear my voice! let every man deal justly with another, speak the Truth, seek the path of true justice and never say, "I need seek no further,"

14 walk in ways of modesty and simplicity, shunning all forms of deceit and hypocrisy,

15 seek earnestly and diligently and surely you will find, selah; but expect no results if you are half-hearted and lukewarm,

16 hear my voice, for I am one who has tasted the waters of Truth at their Source! I come to scatter the seeds of wisdom and enlightenment over the whole Earth,

17 I am a planter of acorns intended to rise up into oak trees of Divinity!

18 do not delude yourselves that because I am among you, I have chosen you above others, I come among the worst not the best, and I am charged to go to all men,

19 yet though I come as an eagle, to strike the foxes who seek to wreck the fowl pen,

20 I come also to salve the wounds of the broken-hearted, and to lead those captive in ignorance to freedom!

21 I am not a prophet of new doctrines, neither do I declare Truth to be a new thing,

22 Truth remains always the same, however she is clothed,

23 I am not a foreteller of the future and do not claim the ability to know the end of any one of you, or even my own,

24 what lies ahead for any one of you is in your own hands.

Chapter 3

1 Some things are certainly revealed to me, and these I must reveal to you, for this is the obligation of a prophet,

2 I come among you not as a miracle worker, but as one charged with the duty of warning you openly,

3 among you are many who make secret mockery of their religion, or who conceal their true beliefs behind a false facade of righteousness, to those I say, beware,

4 awake to Truth! for you are deceived by worldliness!

5 they have failed the test of life, they are victims of its delusions,

6 hear my voice! every man is his own mother, this is Truth, for as a man forms himself, so will he be brought forth!

7 do not reject me, because I differ not from you, I speak in the words of men and act as men act, I make no claim to be more than man,

8 if you say to yourselves, "Why should we listen to this one who

is no more than a man? seeking to change our ways? and undermine the teachings of our fathers?"

9 I say, have I come with guileful tongue? and lips coated with honey? do I wear garments of silk and linen? and eat at tables of luxury?

10 I do not come to speak pleasantries to you, but to declare the harsh and unavoidable Reality!

11 what I bring is not a honeyed drink, but a bitter draught, are these the wares of a false prophet?

12 if I am in error then all I endure is in vain, if I am wrong then on me is the punishment; but I have the assurance of certainty;

13 if the things of which I speak be fabricated by myself, or be the fruits of my imagination,

14 then I am like one who labours without wages, for I toil and suffer without gain,

15 even worse, I damn myself before the judgment seat of Truth!

16 what I have can be any man's, if he is prepared to suffer and endure as I did,

17 do you expect to obtain what I paid for so dearly, for nothing? to know Truth, you must accept my word, or, follow the road I trod, you have the choice,

18 I do not come before you declaring myself the confidant of The Supreme Elohim, the knower of secrets unattainable by others,

19 I do not lay claim to miraculous powers, neither do I pretend to

have the ability to forgive sins, these things are beyond the ability of any man,

20 this I do declare to you:

21 I am no Superior Being, no Angel descended from the Heavens above, I am a man, such as you,

22 will you not hear me as brother listens to brother? will you pay less attention because I am cast in the same mould as yourselves?

23 hear my voice, for I have come to awaken those who sleep! I come to lead the blind! I am the eyes of those who do not see!

24 I am not a beguiler promising soft beds or comfort,

25 I come as a warner against those who promise an easy way, and I raise my voice against any who lull you into indolence by declaring the ability to intercede for you,

26 there is no easy way! and no one can intercede for another! each man is the master of his own fate,

27 as each man plants so shall he garner, and as he moulds himself so shall he come forth, there is always a Day of Reckoning!

Chapter 4

1 Long years I struggled and prepared myself, seeking to discover Truth and the purpose of life,

2 then, the day came when the Truth was revealed,

3 and I saw myself as one seeking for selfish ends, for the

satisfaction and contentment of knowing! I, who should be strong, was weak,

4 so I devoted my full attention to the Instructing Voice,

5 I tested it for Reality and knew it was no delusion,

6 now, I act only upon the knowledge and proofs I have been given,

7 I am not a bearer of idle tales, do you think me such a fool as to sacrifice all I held dear? to give up all I possessed? to come and preach a false doctrine to those who would repay me with nothing but scorn?

8 do you consider me so lacking in wit that I would commit such an act of folly?

9 do not disregard what I have to say, the words I speak were dearly bought! do you treat them contemptuously because it was not you who paid the price?

10 hear and heed! I come to proclaim the Way of Life!

11 I can neither save you from the effects of your own errors, nor remit even the slightest transgression, I can only point the way,

12 I can only offer myself as a guide, I cannot drive you, I cannot carry you, neither can I assume responsibility for your fate,

13 if you are bent under a burden of sorrow, then I will lighten your load!

14 if you are oppressed, I will come to your aid! if you are lonely, then I am your friend! my hand is ever ready to help,

15 all things within my power to give I gladly offer, whether they be of this world or transcending it!

16 but false promises to gain popularity, fair words to make friends, appeasing words to turn away anger, those I cannot give;

17 the Day will come when we shall all stand naked before the Glare of Truth! that Day I do not fear, can the comforting false prophets speak likewise?

18 sons of fools are fathers of fools, if you will not accept these words of Truth, you deny them to your children,

19 revile me as you will, sheep bleat and asses bray, but the stalking wolf makes no reply,

20 I follow my beliefs, you follow yours, me to my end, you to yours;

21 had it been in accord with the Creating Intent, you could all have been born perfect in righteousness!

22 but what would you have been then? mere puppets dangling from the hand above,

23 the Divine Intent was not to create puppets, what end could they serve?

24 The Most High Adonai wants men, men with freewill, capable of decision! free men reaching upwards to Divinity, choosing it of their own accord!

25 you look upon me and say in your hearts, "Can we believe him?" yes! look upon me and see how I live, do I not live by my own words?

26 now, look upon those who declare me to be a false prophet, who are they?

27 are they not those who trample others underfoot in a scramble for power? do they not thrust the orphan aside? and permit the poor to starve in the midst of plenty?

28 who is the less hypocritical one to follow and believe?

29 may the woes of the world descend upon those who pray with their lips, while their hearts remain dead and unmoved!

30 likewise those who display devotion in public places, but turn a hungry man away from their back gate!

31 let them suffer no less who worship in the daylight, but in the darkness of night indulge in whispers of scandal and deceit!

Chapter 5

1 Hear my voice! listen to my words, obey these rules of conduct:

2 If any man names you a liar or treats you as one, have no further dealings with him;

3 keep away from the smooth-tongued man with oily ways, for he is unworthy of your friendship;

4 keep your face unsmiling in the presence of a man who uses vile language,

5 what spews from his mouth is the overspill of the rottenness within, he is empty and weak, and if encouraged, will spread his disease far and wide;

6 all things which really benefit man, whether materially or ruach-ually, and do no harm, are good, and should be encouraged;

7 if a man comes to you and says he has secret knowledge of benefit to man, then hear him fairly, bear with him patiently, for if he is sincere, even though you may derive no benefit and may be told nothing new, his sincerity needs encouragement;

8 though it is well to convert others to the Way of Truth, tread wearily,

9 many will seek to lay snares for you, or to find some hidden vice,

10 but, if you live as your Creator dictates, you will go free, and they will become ensnared!

11 foolish men believe what they want to believe and see what they want to see, leave them to form themselves as they will,

12 the Day will come when they will see themselves as they actually are, and on that Day fear will overcome them, they will not know where to run, all their cunning and trickery will not avail them then,

13 their words of scorn and mockery will rise up within them as bitter bile rises into the mouth,

14 have compassion for them! for on the Dread Day they will stand alone, their waiting companions the uncomforting horrors, skulking just beyond their sight!

15 those who have no desire for Truth will never be convinced of its existence!

16 there are many who do not believe in the existence of The

Supreme Elohim, because they fear to do so, not because it conflicts with their reason or inclinations,

17 hear my voice, listen to my words! I have Books of Kodesh Wisdom giving guidance towards the light! I teach from them, and if they remain hidden, it is to keep them from the hands of despoilers,

18 you who remain with face set towards the darkness of disbelief, go your way,

19 if your affairs appear to prosper better than the affairs of those who walk in the light, do not deceive yourselves,

20 The Supreme Elohim is compassionate and you prosper because He pities you for your future fate!

21 in His mercy, He is granting you an abundance of pleasure in this life, enjoy it while you may!

22 to you who hear my voice, I say, let these things not bother you or appear unjust,

23 it is proper that the just and upright should suffer, for they are the chosen ones to be tested for greater things,

24 the weak horse is never heavy-laden;

25 you who withdraw, closing your ears to my words, who erect a barrier around your hearts so my teachings cannot penetrate, follow your way,

26 you take your road, and I will take mine, but when the gloom closes about you, do not say, "I have been treated unjustly!"

27 if any injustice is done, it will be by yourselves to yourselves,

28 the wickedness you have done will then recoil upon you, the Truth you derided will have caught up with you!

29 laugh if you will, but laugh well, for your laughter will come to an end, beyond it lies an ocean of tears!

30 if my teachings do not stir your hearts to response, they will not be forced upon you,

31 who am I to change the order of things and still your doubts? I have not come to bring assurances, but as a warner, and awakener,

32 many times, I have been tempted to withhold part of my message, knowing you would hold it in scorn,

33 I have been faint-hearted when others have mocked, saying, "Bring down an elohim from Heaven, or disclose the hiding place of treasure and we will believe,"

34 hard is the road of a prophet, and that is all I am, not a conjurer,

35 I speak with the voice of The Supreme Elohim! I serve Him, and to Him is my life dedicated!

36 were I to demand a sign from Him to bolster my own faith, would I not be unworthy of His trust? and a failure as a prophet?

37 a true prophet speaks harsh words, he is known by his unpopularity,

38 you turn from me, saying one to the other, "What does he want of us? where lies his gain?"

39 I ask nothing from you except a receptive mind!

40 I ask no riches, I seek no payment, my reward lies in the knowledge of a duty done, in a clear conscience, in having done my best,

41 were I seeking wealth, or even fame, this is the last way I would set about it,

42 I speak with a true voice, I am no deceiver with some subtle end in view,

43 I make no claim to possessing Kodesh treasures of wisdom, I make no claim to the knowledge of hidden mysteries or great secrets,

44 I am not an Angel, nor an elohim sent direct from Heaven, I am one of your own kind,

45 I am not a hypocrite seeking to curry favour by taking your side against those who ridicule your own views,

46 I stand alone, asking favour of no man,

47 I speak according to my heart! as my heart, so my lips!

48 my words are true, if I did not utter them I would be a coward, and a betrayer of all I hold dear!

Chapter 6

1 I am not the Prophet of Shalom, he is yet to come, wait and listen!

2 do not worship vainly and to no purpose! serve The Supreme

Elohim! for there is none greater to serve, if you think otherwise, you devise false things,

3 take my teachings into your hearts, I offer them gladly, asking no reward,

4 will you not open your hearts and incline towards the light?

5 you demand proof of my prophesy, that I am what I declare myself to be,

6 the proof of a true prophet is in his way of life, have I ever lived otherwise than in accordance with my teachings?

7 false prophets gain worldly things, true prophets suffer unrewarded, without complaint; even then, what they suffer in the sight of men is only a small part of the whole burden;

8 you mock my teachings, declaring them to be false and foolish, you are suspicious of them, what do you fear?

9 be honest with yourselves, is it not because they disturb you? that inwardly, you know their Truth?

10 I have not come to bring you consolation, I come to cause you anxiety! I do not speak words of comfort, but words of urgency!

11 change your path now, before it is too late! the road back is long and tiresome!

12 you may ask me whether it is my desire that you should abandon the worship of your fathers? this is not my desire, retain all that is good and beneficial, reject all that serves no purpose;

13 you accuse me of being too solemn, you say I have lost the ability to laugh, that I set my face against merriment, in all this

you wrong me, for I never set myself against laughter and happiness,

14 in all things there must be balance, laughter and happiness have their place, but they are not things of supreme importance;

15 you say, "Why should we not deal with our possessions and our lives as we wish? they are ours!"

16 I say, no man has sufficient wisdom within himself to know where his benefit lies, therefore he must seek guidance if he be truly wise,

17 which is the wiser? to deal with your lives according to the prompting of inclinations and desires? or to live them in a way most beneficial to yourselves?

18 why then do you reject my teachings or doubt my sincerity? have I asked anything from you except a change of heart?

19 you mock me, saying, "We cannot understand the import of your great teachings," or you deride me, saying, "Were it not that we have pity on your state of madness, we would drive you away from us,"

20 for your sakes I have given up all I once possessed, I have left all I hold dear,

21 can you not spare me a few moments of your time? these are not superficial teachings! can you not spare time to consider them?

22 you say I am no more than a man like yourselves, this is true,

23 you say I am powerless among you, that I remain only because of your benevolence and goodwill,

24 if you think me powerless, you are mistaken, do not think me helpless because I come among you with humility and restraint,

25 had I so desired, my knowledge could have brought me riches and position, instead, I chose to live as I do and follow the road of a true prophet, is this not proof enough of my sincerity?

26 the times are good, there are bountiful harvests and the land is at shalom,

27 men come and go without fear, pleasure and comfort are to be found on every side,

28 it is a bad time for prophets, turbulence and trouble are needed to stir the hearts of men, to lift up their eyes to greater things!

29 when a man is beset with trouble, he turns to ruach-ual things for consolation and help, but no sooner has it passed than he reverts to his former ways,

30 many among you have come forward in a half-hearted manner, and said, "We have heard and believe, we are followers of your teachings,"

31 then the day came when they were called upon to make sacrifices for their beliefs, then, there was a speedy sorting out!

32 my mission is to find those who wish to serve Abba Adonai!

33 the man who pillows his head on a log is more likely to pray than one who lays on a pillow of down;

34 I am not a man gifted with eloquence, and did I come performing miracles, all would follow me, even the hypocrite and evildoer would be among those who walked the road,

35 who then could separate the chaff from the grain? the weak from the strong? those worthy of Divinity, from those who were not?

Chapter 7

1 All creation is upheld by the Torah, and the value of the Torah is revealed in the fact that even The Supreme El does not act against it,

2 the Torah is good, and it must be strictly applied!

3 if men are insincere and shiftless, the performances of miracles will not strengthen their hearts, they are like voyagers at sea: A storm rises and they are distressed, it abates and they rejoice,

4 when the winds roar and the waves mount up, they pray and proclaim their repentance, they profess their intention of living a new life, if saved,

5 yet, when they come safe to land again, they forget all that passed, they return to their previous ways,

6 they commit self-injuring excesses, and deeds of selfishness, only further affliction brings these to an end, can you not understand?

7 hear my voice, those of you who miserably bewail their misfortunes: When troubles beset you and new trials confront you every day, know you are being tested, life itself is a necklace of tests,

8 accept with fortitude whatever test life presents, saying in your heart, when meeting each one, "However this may appear now, it

is for my ultimate good!"

9 you seek miraculous solutions for your problems? do you not understand the nature of freewill, and that miracles are contrary to it?

10 were they part of normal life, your fear of Divine intervention, or reliance upon Divine power, would sap your independence and stifle the expression of freewill,

11 your choice between good and evil would no longer be free, and you would become more of puppets and less of men,

12 so face up to every trial! for only the tests successfully undergone and the good deeds done have lasting value!

13 no two persons have the same abilities and inclinations, therefore, let each man serve The Supreme Elohim according to his endowments,

14 do not try to imitate another in service, for such imitation accomplishes less,

15 follow the road of your own choosing, serve to the best of your ability, live a good life! little more can be required of any man,

16 however, do not close your mind to The Supreme Elohim, thinking that service through earthly skill and ability is enough,

17 what you think and what you believe best, may all be wrong, you may not even know what is for your own good,

18 you were born without being consulted, you cannot direct your lives according to your desires, and you will die, whether you wish it or not,

19 such is earthly life,

20 and likewise, your condition in the afterlife may not accord with your own designs and will! selah;

21 you say, "Death is the end of all things! therefore, let us live as we will!"

22 are you certain? that you can state this as a fact?

23 what do you know of death? the only fact you do know beyond a doubt, is that death is the universal lot of man,

24 therefore exercise caution regarding something you know little about!

25 shed no tears for those who are already beyond the place of tears, can weeping console them? or mourning assist them?

26 what is life? or what is death? that you should grieve for either? they come and go, they merge one into the other,

27 sorrow and joy, pain and pleasure, tumult and shalom, they come and go, they play about man and are gone,

28 they are like winds rustling a tree, they pass, and the tree remains unmoved,

29 life is a lamp-lit room, with two doors leading to the darkness of night.

Chapter 8

1 Hear my voice! I condemn the slanderer, the talebearer, and the hypocrite! they are the inheritors of darkness, the ones destined

for the dismal abyss!

2 I condemn those who amass riches and store possessions against the future, and those weaklings who delude themselves that wealth will shield them against the trials of life!

3 these are times of worldliness, when riches are the lure, the obsession of men,

4 only on the brink of the grave do they see the folly of their ways, then, when it is too late, they cry out in despair, saying, "Grant us just a little more time!" of what value would more time be to them?

5 food which would sustain widows and orphans is thrown by the rich to their dogs, and they say, "This is the natural order of things,"

6 I condemn them, not for their riches, but for what they think,

7 here, the widows and orphans cry, but who will cry beyond the grave?

8 ah, you indolent rich, fatten yourselves up, surely a lean time lies ahead!

9 and do not shift the blame when your just desserts are meted out,

10 you are the guardians of your future, the preparers of your future abode!

11 I condemn the self-deceivers! they say, with hypocritical lying heart, "This may be done, and this is forbidden,"

12 they split hairs, they have a conscience of convenience, they

interpret the message from the formation of a letter,

13 hear my words! heed what I say,

14 do not twist the Truth so that it becomes lies! and say, "These are rules for the conduct of others," at the same time masking your own deeds under a convenient veil of distortion,

15 never make torot for others, which you are unable to keep yourself,

16 are they better than you? if so, let them make torot!

17 I raise my voice against mean-minded men!

18 would there be any justice, were they to share the same fate as the generous and self-sacrificing?

19 I also condemn cowards! when they are told, "Be men, this is your duty!" their hearts quail inside them,

20 their knees tremble, their feet shift, they know their true nature will be revealed and can find no words to avoid their obligations;

21 those, I do not seek as converts, let them go their own way, for if there is hardship or persecution, if the followers of Truth are to be tested for their worthiness to survive and bear the light, where will they stand?

22 the smug, self-satisfied man is also not called upon to follow,

23 if good fortune smiles upon him, he will say, "See what I have been given? I must surely be a worthy man!"

24 the good fortune has been granted in mercy and compassion, his future fate is awful!

25 I condemn the man who says, "I am pure and I am good!" who is he to judge?

26 does the polecat think its own smell bad? does the adder throw away its venom?

27 only the deluded fool says, "I know what is good and what is bad, and need no information on the matter!"

28 when good fortune comes, he says, "I have led a good life, and this is my reward," or "This results from my own efforts,"

29 if misfortune befalls him, he says, "This is the fault of some other," or "This is a chastisement from above,"

30 the Weaver knows the design of the whole tapestry, the threads only the colour in their own part,

31 this life must be viewed together with the life to come if it is to be understood! only The Great Designer can do this,

32 and He metes out success and failure, joy and sorrow, all the tests of life accordingly,

33 heed these words! and heed them well.

Chapter 9

1 If some of you have done wrong and acted against your own future good, whatever it is, the harm is not irreparable,

2 there is still time! how long is unknowable, and that uncertainty is essential,

3 the damage must be repaired by a constant outpouring of good, yet this alone is not enough,

4 for the roots of evil must be torn up within you, felling the tree is insufficient!

5 those who heed my words and follow my teachings are Pilgrims on the Path!

6 they must be resolute and resourceful, for the going is tough, each victory a Pilgrim wins contains the promise of a harder one to follow,

7 every obstacle overcome brings another into view, from birth to death, life is a continual overcoming!

8 I do not speak of profound things, my words are for the ears of unlettered men, I try to speak within the understanding of every man and woman, and according to their capacity,

9 but because of this the enlightenment given to the many, may have no value to the few,

10 even so, there will be those who find it beyond their comprehension,

11 my teachings are many-sided, and therefore, each must interpret them according to his own capacity for understanding,

12 my words are not for those whose minds are pools of stagnation, a pot filled with stagnant water cannot become a receptacle for the flowing waters of wisdom,

13 my words are not for the intolerant and prejudiced, fresh milk cannot be mingled with sour;

14 hear my voice! where are my worldly adversaries? let them come forward and meet me in open discussion before you!

15 why do they keep away? why do they seek refuge behind influential men?

16 it is time to separate the good from the bad, the serviceable from the worthless!

17 the Earth is overloaded with useless things, progress is impeded in a welter of unnecessary things, it is deafened with the clacking of foolish tongues, and overwhelmed in a spate of valueless words,

18 society wallows in the mudhole of a purposeless existence, it must pull itself out or be drawn under and perish,

19 and this can only come about when man obeys the Torot of Life as recorded in the Scriptures!

20 live in accord with your neighbours, for irrelevant quarrelling harms all and benefits none,

21 endure every trial with steadfastness, and in the time between the tests, prepare for the next, never be caught unprepared,

22 many desire fame or greatness, but these come only in accordance with destiny, and if it be destined, they will come unbidden, therefore do not make these your aim in life,

23 those who live a good life, maintaining themselves in uprightness and shunning the ways of wickedness, do this for their own good, they are wise,

24 but would be foolish and hypocritical, were they to hold it was done for the sake of The Supreme Elohim alone, and not for their

own sakes also!

25 some have been given riches in abundance, they lack none of the good things of life, others have nothing, and their burdens are grievous and heavy,

26 I have heard men say, "What kind of Adonai makes this the order of things?" but it is not Adonai! it is man who establishes this as the order of things!

27 The Supreme Elohim will not undertake the tasks of men, neither will He withdraw the tests of temptation when they are placed in the paths of men,

28 the Torah covering the dealings between men judges men with a greater justice than Earth can ever know!

29 it differentiates between the powerless slave who owns nothing and the man abundantly supplied with wealth and possessions,

30 a kind word or drink of water from a man in bondage is of greater value than gold pieces from a man of wealth,

31 a poor man who gives from compassion or comradeship does so in goodness,

32 but the goodness of a rich man giving in consciousness of charity, or from pride in his possessions and position, lacks the same purity, it is tainted,

33 whose goodness has the highest quality? that of the poor man who shares all his food and clothing with a fellow man? or that of the rich man who gives a few pieces of gold from the thousands in his treasury?

34 the same Torah differentiates between the maimed and afflicted and those who are whole and healthy, between the strong and weak, the dull-minded and the keen-minded man,

35 to act according to this Torah on Earth, selah; is to know that each man will be judged according to his ability and means,

36 and the feeling and intent behind an act are what give it value.

Chapter 10

1 I speak again to the cowards, for in these pleasant times who knows where they are? there has been no sorting out,

2 only their loud voices betray them, their love of comfort, their lack of hardihood, their appreciation of womanly things,

3 they say, "Would that times were different, and we had a call to action," but when a matter is placed at issue, when the opposition is aggressive and immovable, they melt like wax images before the heat of fire;

4 there are others, not cowards, who have a point of weakness in their family ties,

5 obligations have an order of precedence which is to be strictly observed, but few men are so unbiased that they can decide such things for themselves,

6 wives and children cause men to stray from the strict path of duty, but for this, the wives and children are to be held blameless,

7 a wife and children are the sun of a man's life, they are almost indispensable to his full development!

8 yet they, like riches and power, are sources of trial, a means of testing, and every man should act in the light of this knowledge, by doing so, his life will be more harmonious and beneficial,

9 he should also bear in mind that his relationship with all his family is judged according to a Torah similar to the one just mentioned: As he treats them, how he acts, so is he judged!

10 the family living in a hovel of poverty is not expected to conform to such a high standard as the one in a place of plenty,

11 that the former does is to its credit, and that the latter fails and its standard falls below the other, is to its discredit, there will be a proper accounting!

12 those who live contentedly, snug in the bosom of their family, safe at home, going placidly about their daily affairs, untroubled by the call of the cause or the demands of duty, shall not be treated or judged like those who sacrifice and serve!

13 the placid and indolent are not judged the same as those who struggle resolutely and endure steadfastly!

14 the constant and the inconstant are not treated alike, their merits are in no way similar,

15 there is a greater recompense of merit for those who turn their back on home comforts than for those who remain content with shalom and placidity,

16 these are times of shalom and prosperity, but are they times of inner stability?

17 those born less fortunately, who have fought in bloody wars, who have been driven away homeless, who have endured famine, imprisonment, or persecution, have learned that mutual suffering

is the cement of humanity,

18 the sweet flowers of friendship and understanding are found in the deserts of despair and distress, not in the pastures of pleasure and prosperity,

19 shalom and prosperity cannot remain with you forever!

20 therefore when trouble and strife descend upon you, as they have in the past, remember that the pattern of life is one of light and shade!

21 happiness and sorrow, success and failure, contentment and strife are sent alternatively among men,

22 that the good may be known from the bad, the strong from the weak, the true from the false, the straight-forward man from the hypocrite, and the selfish soul from the unselfish.

Chapter 11

1 Now, I will speak about deceitfulness, the evil rampant among you! nay, do not seek to drown my words in an avalanche of mockery,

2 honest men do not fear Truth! the Words of Elohim do not beat painfully against their ears,

3 there is no deceit so profound as the deceit of the self-deceived!

4 they are prisoners in a cell of their own building, and they have cast the key into the moat outside,

5 they may hide their true selves from others in this life and think they have done well, but there will be no such deception in the

life to come!

6 some self-deceivers stand before me, half their thoughts proclaiming their goodness, and the others preparing acts of deceit,

7 others say, "But we are good and we are just," and twist the lessons of the Scriptures with their own interpretations, and misquote to comply with their own convenience,

8 they cannot deceive The One Who sees the reflection of their inner image, but they may deceive you, for they put on the face of plausibility,

9 only He sees behind their mantle of goodness displayed to the eyes, and discovers the rottenness hidden underneath! the alms they give, the good deeds they perform, are no more than palliatives to their consciences,

10 they blow themselves up to appear great in the eyes of men, but there is nothing inside except wind,

11 beneath the mortal surface, there is a puny thing, weak and withered, could these only see their future fate they would surely cry!

12 to you who are healthy-minded, I say, keep well away from those self-deceivers, for if they do not corrupt you, they will surely lead you astray,

13 take no notice of what they say, their words are false, seek rather to discover the things hidden in the alcoves of their hearts!

14 some of you who are Pilgrims on the Path will find many seeking to gain your confidence and appearing willing to repudiate their own kind, have no dealings with them,

15 a man who would betray his faith, his race, his nation, his convictions, or his family is a weak reed, from which no support can be expected, and upon which no reliance can be placed;

16 if a man plots your downfall, return cunning with cunning, it is not wrong to slay a snake with its own venom,

17 if you disregard a man who schemes against you, you support his cause;

18 those totally ignorant of the Torah can do little harm, but those who know the Torah and disguise her are dangerous!

19 those who alter the appearance or mask the face of Truth are servants of evil!

20 among them are those who turn the Scriptures to suit their own ends, they say, "This is the true meaning, it is more convenient, less harsh,"

21 or they say, "This we see is written, but we do not strictly obey, it is too exacting to perform, we consider part and discard part,"

22 get rid of them! they confuse the genuine seeker for Truth, and mutilate the Word with their knife of selectivity!

23 Truth cannot be destroyed or changed! she cannot be stripped and displayed to the eyes of men, wisdom and knowledge cannot be trampled underfoot by turning the sword against their upholders!

24 I may not be powerful, I carry no weapons, my voice may be weak, but better men will come in days unborn, and they will sing glad songs of light!

25 the night of ignorance will have its end!

Chapter 12

1 You ask, "Why do the good suffer as well as the bad? why are the innocent afflicted as well as the guilty?"

2 it is because mankind is a single whole, if an arm is wounded the whole body suffers,

3 also, men are not strictly divided into good and bad, guilty and innocent;

4 just as the soul experiences pleasure, so must it experience pain, were it otherwise the pleasure would have no value, can light be known without the contrasting darkness?

5 it is suffering and sorrow, not pleasure and happiness, that have raised man to his present height,

6 pain is unpleasant, agony sometimes unendurable, but they can be accepted and borne by a realisation of their objective, the knowledge that they have a purpose and end,

7 my people, hear my voice, I am your prophet,

8 transmute the dark memories of your sorrows into light seeds of ruach-uality!

9 the pearl of perfect shalom lies in the dregs within the cup of suffering,

10 the haven of happiness lies across the turbulent seas of strife!

11 I speak to the toil-worn! to those heavy-burdened with labour:

12 In the bondage of servitude, you are free! you are not shackled with cravings begotten by idleness,

13 the idle rich are not free, they are slaves to their possessions, they suffer under the lash of their thoughts,

14 labour is not toil and nothing else, its rewards extend beyond worldly things, this is one of the tragedies of the rich who are denied them,

15 I will teach you the Truth, and it will make you free,

16 there is a right way to labour, and there is a wrong way,

17 there is also a way of labour that is full of song and a way that is silent, both play their part,

18 men should choose their form of labour, and in it, they should find contentment and self-expression, then it will not become wearisome,

19 the man who would be happy and contented must seek a form of labour free from anxious thoughts and fanciful desires, it must bring satisfaction and confer benefit;

20 these things have been said before, but I say them again: Do not pursue vain hopes or seek too high a reward, ask only for a just return and remain your own master,

21 it is unwise to seek a position too great for your abilities, by so doing, you burden yourself with a life of straining,

22 be satisfied with whatever fate decrees, and whatever problems perplex you, rise above them,

23 be without jealousy, never envious of another's position,

24 meet success and failure with equal poise, and your days will not be burdensome.

Chapter 13

1 Learn to see the hand of The Almighty Adonai in all things, and make your labour the sacrifice, your toil the offering to Him!

2 with care and diligence, honesty, and skill being your form of worship, you worship well,

3 diligence in the task, a life of moderation, leisure hours filled with service or study, these are proper sacrifices, selah;

4 those who curtail labour and then do nothing useful with the time gained are fools!

5 to abstain from enjoyment to serve beneficial ends is good, so also is dedication of worldly wealth beyond modest needs,

6 giving an honest day's labour for wages, living modestly and frugally, without meanness or harsh austerity, these too are worthy and acceptable sacrifices,

7 it is through sacrifices such as these that The Supreme Elohim is truly glorified!

8 neither contentment in this world, nor happiness in the world to come is for those who do not know the meaning of sacrifice,

9 all good works, all honest labour, all charitable deeds, all payments of full and fair wages, not futile burnings, are worthy

sacrifices!

10 another form of sacrifice is the time devoted to studying the Scriptures!

11 open your hearts to my words! I speak only for your benefit, my voice is not raised for my own amusement!

12 there is much talk about the wickedness and arrogance of the rich,

13 it is not only they who are wicked and arrogant, and no man can be called wicked just because he is rich,

14 wealth does not necessarily serve evil, what matters is how a man deals with the inheritance entrusted to him, not only riches, but also strength, beauty, or talent;

15 search your own hearts before condemning others, it is not only the rich who are idle,

16 each of you, ask yourself how you would fare under the test of riches, and answer honestly,

17 is it certain you are not reviling the rich through envy? are you sure there is no hypocrisy in your hearts?

18 wealth is no light burden, and few, very few survive a severe test!

19 there are others, men of unusual ability, women of great beauty or talent, they, too, often fail; look within before you look without;

20 like those other things, labour is a challenge, the outcome can be a gain or a loss, victory or defeat,

21 the slovenly man who labours only to supply his needs is one on whom life is wasted,

22 the man who declines to utilise mind and limbs to the utmost is no better than the man whose riches permit him to live a life of uselessness,

23 the fault lies with the man, not his money,

24 the enjoyments that flow from worldly things bear within themselves seeds of sorrow to come,

25 worldly pleasures are passing things, and shalom and content are not to be found in them!

26 the man who serves The Supreme Elohim is one who considers the earthly rewards of effort less valuable than the ruach-ual gain,

27 the labour and efforts of Pilgrims on the Path are dedicated to serving mankind! and they reach out for ruach-uality when they find pleasure in their task,

28 therefore labour with zest and dedication, and become a Master of Life!

Chapter 14

1 Even as in all fire there is smoke, so in all things undertaken by men there will be some imperfection, for perfection lies outside this world,

2 the best man can do is strive towards perfection, in whatever he turn his hand to let perfection be the goal!

3 I say to you, seek happiness, enjoy yourselves! life is meant to be more light than shade, I also say, these things cannot be made the whole aim in life, see them in proper perspective,

4 happiness is not the goal of earthly life, it is a reward along the way,

5 but beware, the inclinations of men lure them from the path, I do not speak of things supporting their journey along the way, but of things leading them astray,

6 everyday life is governed by duty and obligation, not happiness and pleasure,

7 to be over-concerned with happiness and contentment is the surest way to unhappiness and restlessness,

8 submission to the Will of The Supreme Elohim is the surest means of avoiding too much suffering and frustration,

9 and knowledge of His Will comes from careful study of the Scriptures!

10 a man's trust in the goodness of The Supreme Elohim must not depend upon the outward circumstances surrounding that man, this is a very important thing to remember,

11 he should try and quell all expectations and preferences, accepting cheerfully whatever comes his way, joyfully enduring whatever destiny bestows, be it joy or sorrow, good or ill,

12 the man who serves best focuses his attention on each step as he travels his path, his only earthly ties being those of love, duty, and obligation,

13 if you are blessed with many gifts, there is no better way to indicate your gratitude than just being quietly and contentedly happy, finding pleasure in even the smallest things!

14 to know the Will of The Supreme Elohim, and do what He Wills, that is the supreme secret of ruach-uality,

15 labouring to fulfil His Torah is to worship with the daily task, a most profitable form of worship,

16 I say, let the Will of The Supreme Elohim be supreme! and subordinate all earthly desires to it!

17 the path of life is on a mountainside, man can ascend or descend according to his inclinations, he can take the hard or the easy way,

18 upwards is the light, downwards the darkness, man has the choice, he goes where he pleases.

Chapter 15

1 I speak to you as a warner, and I warn against the ways of evil men:

2 They are selfish men who are unheedful of the good of others, their thoughts do not extend beyond themselves and their own, they seek to isolate themselves from mankind,

3 they do not know what should be done and what should not be done, they do not understand the nature of good conduct and the path of Truth,

4 they say, "There is no such thing as goodness, mankind has no moral foundation,

5 there is no absolute Truth, there is no Supreme Elohim, there is no Creating Adon,

6 all creation is the result of chance, lust is the only cause of conception,

7 the only purpose of life is an earthly one, we begin and end in the dust!"

8 set in the ways of this belief, these unconscious souls dutifully serve the cause of evil, working, though they know not, for the destruction of mankind,

9 they taint their souls with unrestricted desires and stain them with uncontrolled urges,

10 full of arrogance and deceit, they ride roughshod over the ruach-ual inclinations of others and hold fast to their own dark beliefs,

11 their destructive work is carried on in the name of progress!

12 yet with all they have, they are unhappy and discontented, they are loaded with many unnecessary cares, and their restless thoughts never give them shalom,

13 they fruitlessly seek happiness in sensual enjoyments, in pleasure and gaiety, in the frivolities of life, in drinking and gambling, in luxury and ease, firmly believing they will find it there, that life can offer no more!

14 they are bound fast with fetters of worldliness, they are blind and insensitive to anything else,

15 they seethe within! anger, spitefulness, indignation, and malice

are relieving outlets,

16 they seek refuge in lies and deceit! they hope for relief in outbursts of temper, in lust, sensuality, and in foul language,

17 their only aim is to amass wealth and possessions, or, to live a life of idleness and ease,

18 they say, "What I have I have earned, it is my own, with it I will acquire whatever I wish to satisfy my desires!

19 I have amassed riches, I have come to a high position, men look up to me, I am praised and honoured,

20 I can buy what I desire, I will enjoy life, I am a success, who else is like me?

21 I give charity, I fulfil my obligations, I am sought after by those who need advice and help,

22 I live comfortably, I eat well, I have all I need!"

23 this they say, but are they really happy? and at shalom?

24 they have been deceived by the trap of earthly conditions, they have fallen prey to the alluring phantoms of the senses,

25 they are slaves to their urges and captives of their cravings, they are bound and helpless in a chariot drawn by runaway horses, carried swiftly towards the yawning abyss!

26 weak men, they become drunk with the heady draughts of power and riches, they are carried away by their own arrogance and conceit,

27 they try to turn earthly condition towards serving their own

ends, and struggle futilely against the Torah!

28 willing slaves of arrogance and selfishness, helpless victims in the stormy seas of rage, lust, and violence, these servants of evil hate the Divinity within themselves,

29 they hate and fear the Small Still Voice inside, they stifle it, they smother it under the loud clamour of gaiety,

30 they seek solace in strong wine, in sense-stimulating entertainment, and in ruach-poisoning drugs,

31 stand aside! let them be carried swiftly to the place of sorrow and vain regret!

32 hear my voice, do not fall into the trap of worldliness! do not fall willing victims to the allurements of phantoms!

33 look for Reality! and be satisfied with nothing less than Truth!

Chapter 16

1 Do not reject the Scriptures! study them carefully and you will have a guide through life,

2 they will reveal the right and the wrong, follow their light!

3 do what has to be done, no more is expected of you,

4 heed what I say, for I am your friend,

5 I will speak to you now about the commonplace man:

6 He is one in whom there is neither ruach-uality nor ruach-ual aspiration, he is not righteous, but neither is he really wicked, and

he does not have any ingrained evil qualities,

7 he serves the cause of evil, though he is no more than a mere pawn,

8 no man can stand aside from the conflict, men such as these are unwittingly drawn into the service of evil!

9 the commonplace man has an understanding of good conduct, he is genteel, he is cultured,

10 people like him, he is at ease with them, they seek his company, he is useful to them, as they are to him,

11 but though he is full of worldly knowledge, he has little knowledge or understanding of the Scriptures, or of things transcending earthly existence,

12 he cannot soar into the heights, his feet are planted solidly on the ground, but his wings are undeveloped, he cannot rise above the ordinary,

13 his behaviour is that of the common crowd, he is a commonplace man,

14 he has learnt from earthly experience and associations, what conduct is right and what is wrong to serve worldly ends, this is not enough, to live fully and to good purpose, he must know more;

15 the commonplace woman is like the commonplace man: She moves easily in her earthly environment, but is incapable of raising her eyes above it,

16 she has so much to stir the hearts of men, she can be so desirable, yet, she fails to inspire them, she can goad them on

towards earthly goals, but not to anything greater,

17 she can fan the flame of ambition in her children, but cannot inspire them to look beyond the world;

18 commonplace people have commonplace traits and weaknesses, I will speak of one, revengefulness!

19 an unjustifiable seeking for revenge springs from an inner weakness, the mean and servile person is most addicted to it,

20 malice, like revenge, is a trait of the weak, not of the strong!

21 if someone wrongs you without cause, do not let this disturb your tranquillity of mind, in this way, you will not be unnecessarily upset, but will also be revenged without any need for seeking it,

22 wrongs inflicted by the revenge-seeking man do not disturb the hearts of Pilgrims,

23 the tearing wind and flashing darts of lightning leave the sun and moon untroubled, their anger is vented on trees and things below!

24 the seas of the heart of the revengeful man are in turmoil!

25 you laugh, you mock me, and say, "We prefer life among the commonplace people, for they are easier to get along with, they do not criticise us,"

26 it is true, they will not, if they are unconcerned about their own future, how can they be considerate about yours?

27 you ask, "Why it is that the righteous people keep to themselves? while the wrongdoers are more companionable?"

28 the answer is simple, those who live good lives walk in the light and so do not fear to be alone, they have the companionship of the Ruach,

29 the wrongdoers however walk in darkness, and so have need of company, for they are secretly afraid.

Chapter 17

1 Not long since, one came to me and said, "Prophet, I have offended against the torah of the land, but not against the Torah of the Scriptures, am I blameless?"

2 I tell you this: The torah of the land may extend out beyond the Torah of the Scriptures, but should not conflict with it,

3 if so, the torah outside the Scriptures must also be obeyed,

4 but it is not for me to tell you of these things, if men are content to suffer under bad torot, whose is the blame?

5 the true nature of a nation is revealed in its torot!

6 this I do say: I condemn the torah-makers! who issue unjust and devious decrees, who seek to hide their true intent under a mountain of words,

7 I condemn the unjust torot armed with the sword of legality!

8 I condemn the judges! who spread a legal covering over cunningly laid traps, and snare men in nets made with words, they deceive the ignorant and simple with false masks of legality,

9 Truth and Justice weep outside the courthouse!

10 I condemn also those who stir up strife under protection of the torah, who cause legal mischief or deal in legal deception, to rob the innocent and unwary!

11 wickedness has many faces, but the most hideous is that of those who twist torot to serve selfish ends, or treat the downtrodden with harsh injustice,

12 I speak of these things, but I have not come to change the torah of the land or decide whether they be good or bad, I leave worldly things to worldly men;

13 you say, "Tell us, to which should a man owe greatest allegiance? to the leaders of his nation? or the leader of his faith?"

14 I say this: There is a scale of precedence, and man must serve whatever ranks highest in his heart,

15 the man who obeys his rulers, identifying himself with his people, with their progress, their welfare, their calamities, as though they were his, repenting for their wrongs and rejoicing in their triumphs, that man is a patriot, and patriotism has a proper place,

16 he is above the commonplace man, but not above the man ruach-ually inclined,

17 for ruach-ual things transcend earthly things, as the good of all mankind transcends the good of any nation;

18 in keeping the Torot of the Scriptures, good intent is the main consideration! there must be a complete absence of hypocrisy and deviousness! selah;

19 I speak in conformity with what is written, for if a prophet sets

up a body of torot conflicting with established teachings, or torot claiming to replace them entirely, he is a false prophet!

20 man is the heir to Divinity! he must, however, submit to the Will of The Supreme Elohim, Who is much wiser than man, and this Will is made known through the Torot of the Scriptures!

21 man must not submit abjectly, through fear of punishment or hope of reward, for these things are unworthy of one aspiring to Divinity!

22 there is a ruach-ual value in submission to the Divine Will,

23 where the purpose is obscure and self-discipline required to conform, the value is even greater than where the reason is easily perceived;

24 I am not a man of fancy words, I have lived all my life among wise men and found nothing better for a man than silence,

25 study is not the most important thing, it is deeds! contemplation and speech have their place, but actions shift mountains, while words blow around them!

26 the knowledge that his soul records every word makes a man careful in speech,

27 it is the man whose inner self is wrapped in a mantle of ignorance who keeps no rein on his tongue,

28 if a man antagonises you, never answer him in haste, no reply at all is often an eloquent answer;

29 you ask me concerning marriage, others more able than I have spoken about it, study their words,

30 this I do say: It is not enough for husband and wife to love each other, they must make their love known,

31 a husband does this by showing his wife more respect than to any other woman, is she not the one he chose?

32 or has she been chosen unwisely? if this is so, then it is wrong to make her suffer for it!

33 a wife should be treated with delicacy and care, as the most precious of a man's possessions,

34 as no man expects his wife to defile his home by adultery, he should commit no adultery either,

35 a wise man leaves his wife to be mistress in his house and home, and he provides for her needs to the utmost of his ability!

36 this is the way a wife shows her love for her husband: She is at all times affectionate and womanly, always considerate and gentle,

37 she is careful in managing the household and supervises it diligently, being herself always neat and clean,

38 she never does anything to cause her husband anxiety, she is never wasteful with his earnings,

39 and she pushes aside every thought of other men and never disgraces her house or shows her contempt for her husband by committing adultery.

Chapter 18

1 Now, one asks, "Where shall I seek for Truth?"

2 I say this: They who set about it without hypocrisy will find Truth, no matter where or in what manner they seek, it is never far from men,

3 Truth is everlastingly unchangeable! Earth is false, because it changes and passes away,

4 Truth and The Supreme Elohim are One, because they are Eternal things!

5 things as you see them and things as they really are, are in no way alike, illusion is the environment of Earth, and it deludes the inner eyes with outward impressions,

6 as a needle pricks a blister to let out the water, so does the sharp point of The Scriptures pierce the veil of illusion and let out ignorance;

7 the mind of man is like a pool of water, while it is disturbed, only distorted pictures can be seen,

8 but when it becomes calm and still, the light of ruach-ual Truth is reflected there in all its beauty!

9 the inner being interprets things through a veil of emotion,

10 the man who burns hotly within himself sees the world about him as a fierce fire seeking to consume him,

11 while the man who is calm and quiet within sees all about him as tranquil and shalom-ful!

12 everyone suffers from certain fears in one form or another,

13 the feelings of anxiety, doubt, frustration, and despair are only

normal, but to be overwhelmed by them is a sign of weakness and immaturity,

14 therefore, to those who are fearful and anxious or have doubts, more will be sent! for this is meant to be experienced and overcome, only by this means can man prepare himself for the greater tests ahead,

15 you ask, "How much more sorrow must one suffer to win freedom from sorrow?" there can be no such freedom on Earth,

16 here, the waters of sorrow are drawn from a bottomless well.

Chapter 19

1 I have chosen you from the many because of your eagerness, your attentiveness, your serenity, and your self-discipline, these are the basic qualities required,

2 you must also prove yourselves loyal, and adaptable, strong and trustworthy, intelligent and unselfish, free of all vices and bad traits, efficient, self-reliant, and stable!

3 when I was given my prophethood, I was told to initiate only the worthy persons who had proven their self-mastery and trustworthiness,

4 each of you must snap the knot of the heart,

5 you must study the Scriptures constantly! and apart from these, read words which are beautiful, inspiring, and true!

6 you must constantly strive for tranquillity of heart, for self-control, for self-harmony,

7 be kind and considerate at all times, always maintain purity of thought, and live good lives!

8 practise frugality, but false austerity for your own inner edification is impure,

9 when self-control or self-discipline become self-inflicted torture, or when their intent is to hurt another, then they are servants of evil,

10 however, sacrifices such as I have taught, the kindly acts of everyday living, are not to be abandoned,

11 strive each day to achieve greater self-harmony, for this is the swiftest path upward,

12 the senses and body cravings must be disciplined! otherwise they would assume control,

13 it is not sufficient to be ruach-ually developed, you must ensure that the body is completely controlled by the soul within, therefore, you must not succumb before the rigours of life,

14 you must not pamper yourselves! obtain victory over heat and cold, over the craving for food and drink, over the weaknesses of the flesh, and over the call of comfort,

15 you must cultivate persistence and resolution, for determination is essential on the path!

16 the women must practise all womanly virtues, such as decorum, decency, pity, modesty, sincerity, devotion, purity in all things, cleanliness, and love of love!

17 they must be free of all sensuality, lewdness, and crudeness,

18 they must maintain an evenness of mind through all things, whether pleasant or unpleasant,

19 they must aim for a single outpouring of pure love! a love never straying, never deceptive,

20 they must have contentment of heart, so that they can enjoy solitude, avoiding vain enjoyments and the noisy multitude;

21 the men must seek contentment and calmness within, and outwardly display a steadfast and unruffled front,

22 they must be courageous, generous, truthful, strong in character, and healthy in body!

23 they must cheerfully accept austerity and have the ability to endure privation, solitude, and a rigorous life,

24 they will have a distaste for aggression, for bullying, for the arrogant and haughty, for the cruel, and for the boasters;

25 in men and women, there will be a constant yearning to awaken the soul,

26 there is to be an ideal to be upheld, and a vision to follow!

27 you may practise all things and follow any way of life, consistent with the ruach-ual aims set out in the Scriptures,

28 hating another unjustifiably is wrong, but hatred itself is not necessarily wrong,

29 there is no wrong in hating cruelty, wickedness, arrogance, and many other things of evil!

30 the measure of all things is to be how they effect the sole aim

and purpose of life, the upward flight of man!

31 in seeking contentment and shalom, beware that you do not fall into the pits of complacency, passiveness, and inertia,

32 apathy also sets its trap, and when caught in any of these, you will be doomed to a ruach-ual death!

Chapter 20

1 There are two kinds of people in the world: There are those who must chase enjoyment and pleasure because there is no happiness within them,

2 they are empty and have to suck happiness from people with whom they associate, or from their environment, or have to obtain it by external stimulation,

3 those are the ruach-ually deficient;

4 then there are those who are inwardly happy, they shed joy and contentment,

5 wherever they go they are a lamp of happiness giving out a bright glow which all may enjoy,

6 those can enjoy external things, but are not dependent on them and readily find happiness internally and shalom,

7 they are the ruach-ually healthy;

8 the purpose of earthly life is to experience!

9 therefore be wise enough to understand that though contentment and shalom may be desirable, they are no more than that, they are

not prime objectives,

10 some people are like the uncomprehending butterflies, fluttering aimlessly from flower to flower of sensation and pleasure,

11 then there are the ruach-ually strong, who are like hawk-eyed birds, flying directly towards their objective, riding high above lower creatures, those are the two kinds of people;

12 since they never look within, the ruach-ually deficient lack awareness of the soul, and thus wander aimlessly.

Chapter 21

1 Always seek the beautiful in life, and add to it!

2 turn aside from all forms of vulgarity and crudeness, but it would be better to replace them with graciousness and loveliness,

3 however, do not forget that all too often a man seeking the beautiful, becomes soft, and it is well established that beauty can ruin a man!

4 be a man of few words, this does not mean become dumb, but make your words have value, it means avoid idle chatter,

5 a man can be judged by the company he keeps, so make sure you are always in good company,

6 avoid all persons of bad repute, for they follow a path of destruction!

7 be vigorous and alive, never fearing hard work! no living man can ever fully renounce work or effort, so avoid being numbered

among the dead,

8 be a Master of Life! this is one who has his body and emotions firmly in rein,

9 when hard pressed by tribulations and afflictions he remains steadfast, his mind is never confused,

10 he knows what has to be done, what is expected of him, and does it! he strikes swiftly when action is needed, or just keeps plodding along the path,

11 his mind is clear regarding his duty, he knows his obligations and does not shirk them,

12 and he is always a pillar of strength to his weaker brethren;

13 who are the Masters of Life?

14 when you can ride the stormy seas of sorrow, when you are not overcome by pleasure, when you can control the passions, master fear, discard anger, and whatever comes maintain a quiet and steady manner, you will be a Master of Life!

15 when you can accept all your obligations cheerfully, do your duty at all times, accepting whatever comes be it good or ill, with steadfast heart, remaining calm in the midst of confusion and upheaval, you will be a Master of Life!

16 when you can temper all your desires with prudence, resist temptations to weakness, and bring all urges under control, when you can bring all senses into harmony, control all emotion, overcome the greed for possessions, and smother unwholesome desires, you will be a Master of Life!

17 when you can subdue anger, dispel dismay, never forget where

your duty lies, and be completely free from confusion of mind, you will be a Master of Life!

18 searching their hearts with wisdom, Masters of Life find a stirring response to something greater, and discover the bond of union between man and the Ruach!

19 when the Master of Life knows his true nature and understands the unity of contact, he is freed from all delusion and sorrow, he rises to touch something greater Above!

20 self-control and harmony form the first step towards becoming a Master of Life,

21 harmony, meaning tranquillity within and harmonious relationships without,

22 self-control, means self-control in all things,

23 even an artist must exercise self-control when creating, the tradesman must control his sharp tools and the physician his knife, everything man does requires self-control in one form or another,

24 but the Master of Life has to do more than this, he has to transform his whole life into a creative act, self-control and creativity going hand in hand!

25 only self-control of itself is not enough, it must be subordinated to goodwill and loving kindness,

26 you, my disciples, must become Masters of Life! never regretting the past nor worrying about the future, but always applying yourselves to whatever is in hand at present!

27 the Masters of Life know what are good thoughts and what are

bad thoughts, they know what to tell and what not to tell,

28 they know what to do and what not to do, they know what serves and what does not, what is good and what is bad:

29 If a house is seen to be on fire, this immediately suggests the getting of water or saving whatever may be within,

30 the commonplace man does not know how to act, he acts foolishly or in haste, the Master of Life does not get excited, he keeps his head,

31 he does not stand aside wringing his hands, he does not rush about or get in the way, impeding others,

32 he does not raise his voice, he does not offer futile sympathy, he remains calm, and quietly and efficiently does what needs doing,

33 he takes charge, or, places himself at the disposal of those who are better fitted to assume control!

34 the Master of Life is not bound by fetters the ignorant wear, neither is he guided into ways of darkness by the blind! he is no longer a prisoner of the flesh, but the charioteer of his body!

35 I call upon each of you! take up your burden, and travel the long road leading to mastership of life!

36 the progress of all Pilgrims who have taken this road is indicated by their conduct:

37 The instability has been left behind, the excesses are gone, the demanding desires are dropped,

38 the spitefulness, greed, and conceit have been discarded,

wickedness and malice are thrown aside,

39 one by one they have been sloughed off, as a snake sheds its skin;

40 as Masters of Life, you will call upon others to follow you in the pilgrimage!

41 they will have to be resolute and strong, willing to devote their whole lives to serving the cause of Truth!

42 they will have to study diligently the pages of the Scriptures, and search ever deeper into the inmost recesses of their being,

43 as Masters of Life, you will set an example far beyond reach of the commonplace man,

44 you will be known from others by a profound serenity and resolute steadfastness, just as the commonplace man is distinguished by ignorance, by restlessness, the urge to hide himself in pleasure, and by enslavement to prejudice and emotion;

45 poise and confidence, the marks of real wisdom and knowledge, distinguish the Masters of Life!

46 unsteadiness, shiftiness, unreliability, ever-changing opinions, and fluctuating loyalties distinguish the commonplace man,

47 undue consideration for the outer body and the satisfaction of its desires marks the commonplace man, and his concern for material things is the prime cause of his delusion!

Chapter 22

1 My disciples, heed what I say,

2 be steadfast in heart and mind, cheerfully accepting the trials and tribulations which will beset you!

3 always seek the companionship of congenial and thoughtful fellow wayfarers,

4 develop your soul by contemplation of life, meditation of the Scriptures, and visualisation of the soul's form of beauty and glory!

5 the following are things you must strive against and overcome, so that they are completely banished from your nature,

6 you have heard them before, but they cannot be repeated too often:

7 All forms of anger, recklessness, cruelty, and boastfulness,

8 all tendencies towards falsehood, deceit, or dishonesty, or towards lewdness, obscenity, or lust,

9 fornication, seduction, and the degradation of women are forbidden,

10 cheating, insincerity, gossiping, slander, and talebearing are unworthy of you,

11 such things as an unforgiving nature, moral weakness, cowardice, instability, irresolution, fickleness, and intemperance are to be eliminated,

12 undue love of comfort, of worldly or sensual pleasures, and all forms of uncleanliness in mind and body must be overcome!

13 there is much talk among you concerning the nature of

worship, understand this, true worship is seeking to unite the ruach below with the Ruach Above,

14 to do this, you must have a heart purged of all evil thoughts, a tongue undefiled by falsehood or tainted with deceit and hypocrisy, and a life free of all malice and hatred,

15 even this is not enough! for you must have a life filled with love and good deeds, only when in this state are you fit to worship!

16 as true disciples, you must spend your whole conscious life in purposeful and constructive thinking, you must be doers and not dreamers!

17 when you withdraw into the silence to worship, remember the great jewels of prayer: Serenity, purity, and trust!

18 how many of you have hesitated because you feared the opinions of others? the entreaties of loved ones? or the thoughts of possible suffering and discomfort?

19 I have spoken of discomfort, this I say again, too much comfort is not for you! neither should you sleep too much or too little,

20 you must overcome all tendencies towards sloth and carelessness, for these will sap your ruach-ual stamina;

21 do not be impatient for advancement, slow progress is often the best,

22 if someone breaks a hatching egg before its time, no chick will emerge, but when the time is ripe, the shell will be broken from within, and a healthy chick will arrive to life,

23 so it is with the awakening soul, let it emerge from within of its own accord!

24 but until you have purged your hearts of all impurities and washed away all the worldly filth, you cannot even set foot on the lower rung of the ladder leading to enlightenment and ruach-ual growth.

Chapter 23

1 You will choose candidates for discipleship who may become Masters of Life!

2 they must be calm and wise, recognising what is real, desirable, important and true, from what is false, illusive, trivial and unworthy of attention,

3 they must be ones who have overcome worldliness and are aware of Truth, they have no inclinations towards anything not actively assisting them in the search,

4 they must not be weak of character, neither must they be seeking a refuge!

5 the Kodesh Scriptures are not to be swallowed as one does a medicinal compound, they are to be assimilated slowly and digested with reason and experience,

6 never forget, it is the meaning, not the mere form of words in the Kodesh Scriptures which is of value,

7 a silken mantle may look better than a coarse woollen one, but which serves best in providing warmth?

8 also, keep in mind that the Scriptures are guides, they cannot

undertake the hard work nor assume the burden,

9 the purpose of the Kodesh Scriptures is to show men what life should be, how they should be governed, how they should conduct themselves, what they should keep and what they should discard,

10 these are the Scriptures of those who follow the Great Path of the True Way, they are not for the mocker, the unbeliever, the man of worldly affairs or the evildoer,

11 nor men who are satiated with worldly learning, who have fallen into the pit dug by their own books!

12 though the Truth within the Kodesh Scriptures is unalterable, can never change, the revelation can always be interpreted according to man's progress,

13 the hidden Truths are to be made available to man whenever he is ready!

14 the ruach-ual man who is truly awakened sees much more in the text than the commonplace man, who may see no more than mere letters and words,

15 yet words are a forest in which man can easily lose his way, fine sentences and a grand manner of expression may just be a lure and a covering for the pit and stake!

16 as there are those who talk about ruach-ual things, but do no more than weave a web of words to trap the unwary!

17 to derive benefit from a bottle, the contents must be taken, merely reading the inscriptions will effect no cure,

18 my disciples, read the Kodesh Scriptures diligently! and never

abandon your work and studies,

19 for to do so when you are struggling to cross the stream of life shows lack of resolution, and it achieves nothing, you will sacrifice your own self-assurance and your inspiration will be lost;

20 never forget, these Words are not fair weather friends, they are not things of feathers to blow away before a slight wind, they are stones in a solid causeway, firm and reliable under all conditions,

21 take these Kodesh Scriptures as your daily guide, make them your advisor whenever a problem arises!

22 unless they are put into practice, they remain valueless, just things to be thought about in idle moments,

23 the Inspired Writings are the mid-wife and nurse of the soul!

24 men should never indulge in argument or discussion as to the form and nature of The Supreme Elohim, this is folly, for an understanding of this is beyond even the awakened mind,

25 remember that three things must be brought together in combination: The Kodesh Scriptures, the wise instructor, and the eager and diligent pupil;

26 some awaken the soul by meditation, sometimes it is awakened through a vision, in some it awakens through good works, in others through labour,

27 it can be awakened by creativity and love, there are many means to suit the numerous conditions of men,

28 none will ever find words adequate to describe it to others,

29 so wonderful is the state of a newly awakened soul, so delightful the experience of sudden realisation, that none who has known it will ever forget!

30 there is no thought except a deep awareness of life, of being,

31 there is a sense of deeper reality than that of ordinary consciousness,

32 faith in the reality of the soul then gives way to certainty and assurance in the reality of The Supreme Elohim,

33 this awakened soul can now live life on Earth with certainty! for how can any man doubt the greatest experience of his life?

The Lived Religion - Book 10 - The Son of Elohim

Chapter 1

1 Behold, this land is a chosen land,

2 out of its womb shall come the Child of Truth, which shall die and rise again to lead men in the struggle to glory!

3 in the day of his rising, the Earth will be distressed and know it not,

4 nor will it open its arms to the Child, which will go unrecognised, and even be despised and mocked,

5 yet, in that day will be produced a salve to heal the scars of mankind!

6 in that day, when men shall have forgotten the way of righteousness and turned from Truth, the light will come unto them!

7 My Son, take not unto yourself the blame for the iniquity of these perverse people, leave them to steep in the brew of the wickedness which they have prepared for themselves,

8 for there is a point beyond which My Administrator is not required to go,

9 leave the wicked, and gather the select few unto yourself! for thus it shall ever be, many will cry at the gates, but few shall enter,

10 abandon the misled to their false shrines, for the Day will dawn when all these shall be dust borne away on the wind!

11 even then, the words of Truth shall remain unto men,

12 go, cherish the few! hide the Kodesh things in places where they shall be least sought,

13 choose well those who are of one thought with you, a roof is better supported upon a few sound pillars than on many unstable ones,

14 to you is given command of men, as He Who Fathered you is given command of ruchot,

15 those men from whom you incline your head shall be removed from out of your sight, and they shall become lost and restless souls!

16 "O Great Adonai, what can I do? how shall Your servants be saved?

17 what shall be done unto those who have profaned You?

18 what can I do to turn back the rising waters of iniquity and temper the wild winds of wickedness?

19 how can the black cloud of ignorance be lifted?

20 what shall be the just reward of those who have slain the faithful?"

21 concern yourself not with those who have persecuted you, leave them to follow the path of their own choice, vengeance is with Me! I will measure without stint,

22 justice never sleeps and never forgets!

23 the reward of the wicked awaits them! in the Great Hall, justice will speak the final word!

24 My Son, your Abba Adonai, I Who Am, chooses you as the sower of seeds,

25 I Who Am will guide your steps, and will open a door in the barrier that you may hear My voice,

26 let your eyes now see, and, behold, I Am Who I Am!

Chapter 2

1 "Why must the ignorant suffer dire consequences? and why is man not more fully warned?"

2 the ignorant do not suffer because they are ignorant, for that is the state into which they were born,

3 they suffer because they are content to remain in that state, and have chosen to take the easy road of effortlessness,

4 the consequences of ignorance alone are not so dire, it is wickedness, chosen either deliberately or unthinkingly, that damns a man!

5 behold, what he suffers is not a punishment, but the natural consequence of his actions; if a man places his hand upon a hot iron and is burnt, the pain is not a punishment, but the consequence of his actions,

6 if a man cuts himself, he must expect to bleed and if he walks through mud, he cannot expect to remain unsoiled;

7 those who seek refuge in the darkness do so not because they

are condemned to suffer in this manner, but because it is the only place in which such as they can live,

8 the worm does not seek the sunlight, or the leech find refuge in anything except slime,

9 all things are drawn into conditions with which they have an affinity, that is a Torah of Nature, as well as a Greater Torah!

10 man is sufficiently warned, for the light has never been denied those who seek it earnestly, and everything about him proclaims the Torah of Affinity,

11 I have not turned away from My children! My children have turned away from Me! by disobeying My Torot,

12 this cry will echo down through the generations of man: "My Elohim, why have You deserted me?" and it will come from those who have deserted their Elohim!

13 yet the day is not far distant when many shall give ear to words of wisdom, for if their ears are stopped, they are lost;

14 men have said, as they will say throughout the ages, "Why, if El be Almighty, can He not create perfection immediately?

15 why does He not create beings having the knowledge of Divine Love forthwith?

16 why have Earth? with all its trials and tribulations?"

17 know this, what appears to you as ages in time is to Me but a flash of thought in a moment of Eternity,

18 I breathed in, the hosts of Earth were not, I breathed out and the hosts of Earth were, I breathe in and they are no more!

19 all things exist within the Eternal One,

20 and that which men know as the span of time, is the act of creation!

21 mark the flight of an arrow from the hands of a bowman: It flies from the bent bow, time passes, then it finds its mark,

22 but to Me, the arrow leaves the bow and strikes the mark together; distance, time, and change are not with Me!

23 once I, your Adon, was not apart from man, My offspring, now I am veiled from his sight,

24 not because I have willed it so, but because man has chosen to bring this about!

25 the barrier between us grows ever more dense, as man wantonly spurns his birthright,

26 henceforth it may be penetrated by long and arduous preparations, and even then those who would do so must know this key:

27 Though there is a barrier between us, it is not impervious to the sincere prayers of a pure heart! this, all men should know,

28 as for you My Son, your days are numbered, you are now no more than the basket holding the seeds which will be strewn and sown by other hands,

29 I come to you, not because of your preparation, but because your Elohim is ever ready to incline towards men,

30 though many things of which I have spoken are not for the ears

of men, for such knowledge, freely bestowed, would not benefit them,

31 many things are beyond their present understanding,

32 let these things therefore be recorded unto the generations of men yet unborn,

33 men are now as children and must learn again as children, being taught childish tales.

Chapter 3

1 The man who has recognised his true nature has already stepped into the domain of ruach-uality,

2 but the man who has craved only for things pleasing to the mortal body and been led astray by carnal urges, is lost, and wanders aimlessly in the darkness of moral wastes,

3 his doom is to be devoured by damnation, the predator of these wastes!

4 when I, the Supreme Elohim, communicated with man, the message was that he should multiply and cover the Earth,

5 man was told to never forget that he was the custodian of his race, and the designer of his earthly dominion,

6 he was also told that submission to carnal desires meant ruach-ual death,

7 and that love is a lady worthy of the greatest respect, and not a menial serving maid attending to the demands of a master!

8 those were the things man was told, but he gave heed only to the first!

9 you call upon Me as Abba Adonai, nor do you err in this,

10 yet I am the Hidden Adon! the El of Secret Manifestation! the Wronged Elohim! the Betrayed Elohim! the Disappointed Elohim!

11 I am the Adon who sought to give Love Divine to men by making them My heirs, making them partakers of Divinity, co-creators with Me!

12 but men spurn their birthright! not through wickedness alone, but through their weakness and love of pleasure,

13 therefore, the love once offered cannot now be displayed in all its glory,

14 it cannot be revealed in its beauty, it must now be leavened with severity and chastisement,

15 this, so that those who are the inheritors of Divinity may return to it with undiminished powers! but, purged of their weaknesses and love of unprofitable pleasure!

16 this you should know, that men may know: Divinity of itself is not a created thing, and cannot be bestowed as a gift,

17 it comes as the crown of achievement!

18 I, The Almighty Adon, Who, by taking thought, can create ten thousand worlds, say this.

The Lived Religion - Book 11 - The Destroyer

Chapter 1

1 The day of the Destroyer will come again! and the land shall be laid waste!

2 it will strike out of Heaven at a time when there is prosperity and plenty, though the minds of men shall be perplexed,

3 it will be a time when men worship the works of men, and say, "There is nothing greater than these!"

4 when women are as men and men as women,

5 when the hearts of men are in turmoil and all men seek pleasure and gain,

6 when craftsmen are inefficient and workmen are idle, and all men seek ease and comfort,

7 be alert and strong my friends! be ready for the day of the next visitation! when doom reaches down from the skies and man is blasted with irresistible power!

8 then, elohim and men intermingled will do battle, and there will be great carnage on that catastrophic day! when war is waged in the red-hued darkness amid mighty blast!

9 that is the time of which it is written, "Fire shall leap forth from the heart of a stone!"

10 in a scroll of the past in our keeping, it is said, "The generations passed, and a vast amount of knowledge and wisdom was accumulated and preserved in purity, it was the heritage of

mankind!

11 but though man had learned to cherish the light of Truth and walk wisely with it, nevertheless, then as now, false priesthoods flourished,

12 they pandered to the carnal desires of the undeveloped, and exploited the weaknesses of the ignorant,

13 their iniquity built up a vast weight of evil in the Netherworld, which projected itself into the material of Earth, so that the powers which upheld it became unstable,

14 this caused all the southern part of the Old Land to sink down into heaving waters!

15 the disaster was brought about through the ascendance of evil, rites which awakened the dead were rife among the carnal-minded and ignorant,

16 while those who remained steadfast on the harder road of ruach-ual development, had fixed their eyes on the light ahead, ignoring the pitfalls at their feet,"

17 it was then even as now, will men ever learn?

18 this was the aspect of the disaster, as written in the scroll:

19 "There were openings in the land from which evil vapours poured forth as a mist, descending upon the people like a mantle, these spread out and covered the whole face of the land,

20 the tongues of the people were stopped, and they became dumb with fear,

21 the ground trembled beneath them, and great tongues of flame

shot up! the whole land heaved and rocked like an ocean wave!

22 as it rose and fell, groaned and shook, the fires which strove beneath burst forth to be met with shafts of lightning striking down from Heaven!

23 a thick black cloud of smoke filled the land, and men were smothered in dust,

24 as the setting sun rested on the horizon, it could be but dimly seen beneath the cloud as a fiery red ball, when it had gone, a grey dense darkness prevailed, lit only by great sheets of lightning,

25 before the dawn, waters broke heavily over the land, sweeping it clean!

26 the plains and cities were covered! and new shores formed around the mountains,

27 the waters mounted up until all that moved and lived was covered! the south land was submerged! mountain tops alone remained above the rush of uplifted torrent,

28 whirlwinds blew and brought cold winds which cleared away the dust and debris,

29 mudbanks were formed, and a mountain mouth remained open to spew forth vile vapours,

30 during one long, awful night, the doomed land was torn apart, and the southward land sank out of sight forever!

31 behold, in the days long gone down into dust, the Destroyer came to Earth and poured out his wrathful breath so that men were burnt,

32 the evildoers were swept away by the waters, and the wicked ones were swallowed up in the fires!

33 the days of the years were shortened and the times of all things altered,

34 the seasons were turned around, so that the seed rotted within the soil, and no green shoots came forth to greet the day,

35 all buds withered upon the vines, the land lay dead under its grey shroud!

36 the moon changed the order of her ways, and the sun set himself a new course, so that men knew not where they were and all were afflicted,

37 the stars swam in a new direction, and the whole order of things was changed!"

38 perhaps nations, like men, grow old and decay?

39 my land is old, a hundred and twenty generations have passed through it since the Great Adon brought light to men,

40 four times the stars have moved to new positions,

41 twice the sun has changed the direction of his journey,

42 twice the Destroyer has struck Earth,

43 and three times the Heavens have opened and shut.

Chapter 2

1 It was the Wildland Cultivators who gave this tale to our Housebuilding Forebears, but the generation of its happening is lost:

2 In those days, harvest followed winter without change, but, it came about, that looking up into a darkling night sky, they saw a strangely formed moonchariot overhead! which passed away into the rosy dawning of a new-born day,

3 but then, at the night end of the skyroof, appeared the dread figure of the Destroyer! revealing itself to the eyes of wondering men!

4 then as it crawled out into the brightness, the foul breath of the nightcomer newly sprung from the dark depths of its unearthly lair, spread across the brightening face of Heaven, like an evil grey veil,

5 and even the ever-fearless sun withdrew to gird himself in red war armour,

6 the fastbeating hearts of men first shrivelled with despair at the fearsome sight, then rose, while their throats responded with glad cries! as the moonchariot came back over the dim horizon!

7 there, riding the battlebar, flaming sword held high, was the bright beloved figure, its fair hair strung out behind, as it flew towards the hellfigure!

8 they met in an awful, hell-echoing clash with the noise of ten thousand rolling thunders, and men bold enough to look were stricken with blindness! and uncovered ears were deafened forever!

9 cold moontears were shed by the fang- and claw-torn champion of mankind,

10 while the hellish Destroyer drooled white cinders, which, if they touched the skins of men below, raised evil weals,

11 the unearthly foemen fell apart, and hurled great self-created rocks at each other, as onlookers below dashed for protective shelter as they howled down out of the sky above!

12 the very Earth, herself immovable, was sickened with fear, and her bowels became loosened with dread, her belly trembled before the awful sight,

13 and men, looking anxiously to the sun, were dismayed to see his constant change of garb, from red to blue, then to yellow, then green, then brown!

14 Earth opened her groundmouth and roared earcracking protests, while her whole comforting body shook in fear under the gloomy battle of the shadowforms above,

15 men and beasts were drawn together in a strange brotherhood of fear, none doing harm to another,

16 those hardy enough to maintain a watch on the combat saw the flashing chariot crush the writhing body of the nightcomer! selah; and then saw its vile black blood, thick like resin, fall upon the bosom of Earth,

17 where the blood fell, flames sprang up!

18 then, the fear-heated, blood-despoiled body of Earth was cooled and refreshed by soothing moontears, shed in comforting relief, as she drove back towards her hidden abode in the recesses of Heaven!

19 this is the tale of the skyfight, but whether it happened before

or after the generation of the floodtale, none now truly knows,

20 it concerns the Doomdragon, which has come more than once, and will come again!

21 and the last music mankind will hear, is the shrill, throbbing notes of the Doomsong.

Chapter 3

1 Men forget the days of the Destroyer,

2 only the wise know where it went, and that it will return in its appointed hour,

3 it raged across the Heavens in the days of wrath! and this was its likeness:

4 It was as a billowing cloud of smoke, enwrapped in a ruddy glow, not distinguishable in joint or limb,

5 its mouth was an abyss from which came flame, smoke, and hot cinders!

6 when ages pass, certain Torot operate upon the stars in the Heavens, their ways change, there is movement and restlessness, they are no longer constant, and a great light appears redly in the skies;

7 when blood drops upon the Earth, the Destroyer will appear, and mountains will open up and belch forth fire and ashes!

8 trees will be destroyed and all living things engulfed!

9 waters will be swallowed up by the land, and seas will boil!

10 the Heavens will burn brightly and redly, there will be a copper hue over the face of the land, followed by a day of darkness,

11 the people will scatter in madness! they will hear the trumpet and battlecry of the Destroyer, and will seek refuge within dens in the Earth,

12 terror will eat away their hearts, and their courage will flow from them like water from a broken pitcher,

13 they will be eaten up in the flames of wrath! and consumed by the breath of the Destroyer!

14 thus it was in the days of heavenly wrath, which have gone, and thus it will be in the days of doom, when it comes again,

15 the times of its coming and going are known unto the wise,

16 these are the signs and times which shall precede the Destroyer's return:

17 Men will fly in the air as birds and swim in the seas as fishes,

18 men will talk shalom one with another, hypocrisy and deceit shall have their day, women will be as men and men as women, passion will be a play thing of man,

19 a nation of soothsayers shall rise and fall, and their tongue shall be the speech learned,

20 a nation of torah-givers shall rule the Earth, and pass away into nothingness,

21 one worship will pass into the four quarters of the Earth,

talking peace and bringing war,

22 a nation of the seas will be greater than any other, but will be as an apple rotten at the core, and will not endure,

23 a nation of traders will destroy men with wonders and it shall have its day,

24 then, shall the high strive with the low, the north with the south, the east with the west, and the light with the darkness,

25 men shall be divided by their races, and the children will be born as strangers among them,

26 brother shall strive with brother and husband with wife,

27 fathers will no longer instruct their sons, and the sons will be wayward,

28 women will become as the common property of men and will no longer be held in regard and respect,

29 then men will be ill at ease in their hearts, they will seek they know not what, and uncertainty and doubt will trouble them,

30 they will possess great riches, but be poor in ruach!

31 then will the Heavens tremble and the Earth move! men will quake in fear, and while terror walks with them, the heralds of doom will appear!

32 they will come softly as thieves to the tombs, men will not know them for what they are, men will be deceived, the hour of the Destroyer is at hand!

33 in those days, men will have the Great Book before them,

wisdom will be revealed, the few will be gathered for the stand, it is the hour of trial!

34 the dauntless ones will survive!

35 the stouthearted will not go down to destruction!

36 Great Adonai of All Ages, alike to all, Whose wisdom sets the trials of man, be merciful to our children in the days of doom!

37 man must suffer to be great, but hasten not his progress unduly,

38 in the great winnowing, be not too harsh on the lesser ones among men; even the son of a thief has become your scribe;

39 O you, who watch for the Destroyer, how long will your enduring vigil last?

40 O mortal men, who wait without understanding, where will you hide yourselves in the dread days of doom? when the Heavens shall be torn apart? and the skies rent in twain?

41 in the days when children will turn grey-headed?

Chapter 4

1 Hearken to the history of the great flood of waters, when the salt seas rose and covered all the land:

2 Men were warned beforehand by the shortening of the days of the years, and the five days now added to the days of the year are days of sorrow for the alteration of things;

3 it is said that seven days before the coming of the waters the sun

appeared in a different quarter,

4 then, with the dawning, men saw an awesome sight!

5 there, riding on a great black rolling cloud, came the Destroyer, newly released from the confines of the sky vaults! and it raged about the Heavens! for now was its time of judgment!

6 the beast with him opened its mouth and belched forth fire, hot stones, and a vile smoke!

7 it covered the whole sky above, and the meeting place of Earth and Heaven could no longer be seen,

8 in the evening, the places of the stars were changed, they rolled across the sky to new stations, then, the floodwaters came,

9 the floodgates of Heaven were opened and the foundations of Earth were broken apart!

10 the surrounding waters poured over the land and broke upon the mountains,

11 the storehouses of the winds burst their bolts asunder, so storms and whirlwinds were loosed to hurl themselves upon the Earth!

12 in the seething waters and howling gales all buildings were destroyed, trees were uprooted, and mountains cast down!

13 there was a time of great heat, then came a time of bitter cold,

14 the waves over the waters did not rise and fall, but seethed and swirled, and there was an awful sound above,

15 the pillars of Heaven were broken and fell down to Earth!

16 the skyvault was rent and broken! the whole of creation was in chaos! the stars in the Heavens were loosened from their places, so they dashed about in confusion!

17 it appeared as a revolt in the Heavens, and a new ruler appeared there and swept across the sky in majesty! selah;

18 those who had not laboured at the building of the great ship and those who had mocked the builders came quickly to the place where it was lying,

19 they climbed upon the ship and beat upon it with their hands, they raged and pleaded, but could not enter inside, nor could they break the wood,

20 as the great ship was borne up by the waters, it rolled, and they were swept off, for there was no foothold for them,

21 the ship was lifted by the mighty surge of waters and hurled among the debris! but it was not dashed upon the mountainside because of the place where it was built,

22 all the people not saved within the ship were swallowed up in the midst of raging confusion! and their wickedness and corruption was purged away from the face of the Earth!

23 approaching that day, all things became still and apprehensive, for Elohim caused a sign to appear in the Heavens, so that men should know the Earth would be afflicted, and the sign was a strange star,

24 the star grew and waxed to a great brightness and was awesome to behold, it put forth horns and sang! being unlike any other ever seen,

25 so men, seeing it, said among themselves, "Surely, this is El appearing in the Heavens above us!"

26 the star was not El, though it was directed by His Design, but the people had not the wisdom to understand,

27 then, El manifested Himself in the Heavens! His voice was as the roll of thunders, and He was clothed with smoke and fire!

28 He carried lightnings in His hand! and His breath falling upon the Earth, brought forth brimstone and embers!

29 His eyes were a black void, and His mouth an abyss containing the winds of Destruction!

30 He encircled the whole of the Heavens, bearing upon His back a black robe adorned with stars!

31 such was the likeness and manifestation of Almighty El in those days, awesome was His countenance! terrible His voice of wrath!

32 the sun and moon hid themselves in fear, and there was a heavy darkness over the face of the Earth.

Chapter 5

1 This is the thing which will be seen,

2 this is the terror your eyes will behold,

3 this is the form of destruction that will rush upon you:

4 There will be a great body of fire, with a glowing head with many mouths and eyes ever-changing,

5 terrible teeth will be seen in formless mouths, and a fearful dark belly will glow redly from fires inside,

6 even the most stouthearted man will tremble! and his bowels will be loosened! for this is not a thing understandable to men,

7 it will be a vast, sky-spanning form, enwrapping Earth, burning with many hues within wide open mouths,

8 these will descend to sweep across the face of the land, engulfing all in the yawning jaws!

9 the greatest warriors will charge against it in vain, the fangs will fall out, and lo, they are terror-inspiring things of cold hardened water,

10 these great boulders will be hurled down upon men, crushing them into red powder!

11 as the great salt waters rise up in its train and roaring torrents pour towards the land, even the heroes among mortal men will be overcome with madness,

12 as moths fly swiftly to their doom in the burning flame, so will these men rush to their own destruction!

13 the flames going before will devour all the works of men! the waters following will sweep away whatever remains!

14 the dew of death will fall softly, as a grey carpet over the cleared land,

15 and men will cry out in their madness, "O whatever being there is! save us from this tall form of terror! save us from the grey dew of death!"

16 the dark times began with the last visitation of the Destroyer, and they were foretold by strange omens in the skies, all men were silent! and went about with pale faces.

Chapter 6a

1 The leaders of the slaves stirred up unrest, and no man raised his arm against them!

2 they foretold great events of which the people were ignorant, and of which the temple seers were not informed!

3 these were days of ominous calm, when the people waited for they knew not what, the presence of an unseen doom was felt, and the hearts of men were stricken,

4 laughter was heard no more, and grief and wailing sounded throughout the land, even the voices of children were stilled, and they did not play together, but stood silent,

5 the slaves became bold and insolent, and fear walked the land,

6 women became barren with terror, they could not conceive, while those with child aborted, and all men closed up within themselves;

7 the days of stillness were followed by a time when the noise of trumpeting and shrilling was heard in the Heavens!

8 the people became as frightened beasts without a herdsman, as asses, when lions prowl without their fold,

9 the people spoke of the Elohim of the slaves, and men said, "If we knew where this Elohim were to be found, we would sacrifice

to Him!"

10 but the Elohim of the slaves was not among them, He was not to be found within the swamplands or in the brickpits,

11 His manifestation was in the Heavens for all men to see! but they did not see with understanding, nor would any of their elohim listen, for all were dumb because of the hypocrisy of men!

12 the dead were no longer sacred and were thrown into the waters,

13 those already entombed were neglected and many became exposed, they lay unprotected against the hands of thieves;

14 he who once toiled long in the sun, bearing the yoke himself, now possessed oxen,

15 he who grew no grain now owned a storehouse full,

16 he who once dwelt at ease among his children now thirsted for water,

17 he who once sat in the sun with crumbs and dregs was now bloated with food, reclined in the shade, his bowls overflowing!

18 cattle were left unattended to roam into strange pastures, and men ignored their marks and slew the beasts of their neighbours,

19 no man owned anything,

20 the public records were cast forth and destroyed, and no man knew who were slaves and who were masters,

21 the people cried out to the Pharaoh in their distress! but he stopped his ears, and acted like a deaf man;

22 there were those, who spoke even before Pharaoh, saying it was their Elohim Who was hostile towards the land,

23 therefore the people cried out for their blood to appease It!

24 but it was not these strange priests who put strife in the land instead of shalom, for one was even of the household of Pharaoh, and walked among the people unhampered.

Chapter 6b

1 Dust and smoke clouds darkened the sky and coloured the waters upon which they fell with a bloody hue,

2 plague was throughout the land, the river was bloody, and blood was everywhere,

3 the water was vile and men's stomachs shrank from drinking, those who did drink from the river vomited it up, for it was polluted,

4 and the dust tore wounds in the skin of man and beast;

5 in the glow of the Destroyer, the Earth was filled with redness,

6 vermin bred, and filled the air and face of the land with loathsomeness,

7 wild beasts, afflicted with torments under the lashing sand and ashes, came out of their lairs in the wastelands and caveplaces and stalked the abodes of men,

8 all the tame beasts whimpered, and the land was filled with the cries of sheep and moans of cattle,

9 trees throughout the land were destroyed and no herb or fruit was to be found!

10 the face of the land was battered and devastated by a hail of stones! which smashed down all that stood in the path of the torrent!

11 they swept down in hot showers, and strange, flowing fire ran along the ground in their wake!

12 the fish of the river died in the polluted waters,

13 worms, insects, and reptiles sprang up from the Earth in huge numbers,

14 great gusts of wind brought swarms of locusts which covered the sky,

15 as the Destroyer flung itself through the Heavens, it blew great gusts of cinders across the face of the land!

16 in the gloom of a long, restive night, spread a dark mantle of blackness, which extinguished every ray of light,

17 none knew when it was day and when it was night, for the sun cast no shadow,

18 the darkness was not the clean blackness of night, but a thick darkness in which the breath of men was stopped in their throats,

19 men gasped in a hot cloud of vapour! which enveloped all the land and snuffed out all lamps and fires!

20 men were benumbed and lay moaning in their beds, none spoke to another or took food for they were overwhelmed with

despair,

21 ships were sucked away from their moorings and destroyed in great whirlpools,

22 it was a time of undoing!

23 the Earth turned over as clay spun upon a potter's wheel!

24 the whole land was filled with uproar from the thunder of the Destroyer overhead! and the cry of the people!

25 there was the sound of moaning and lamentation on every side as the Earth spewed up its dead!

26 corpses were cast up out of their resting places, and the embalmed were revealed to the sight of all men!

27 pregnant women miscarried and the seed of men was stopped,

28 the craftsman left his task undone, the potter abandoned his wheel and the carpenter his tools, and they departed to dwell in the marshes,

29 all crafts were neglected, as the slaves lured the craftsmen away,

30 the dues of Pharaoh could not be collected, for there was neither wheat nor barley, goose nor fish,

31 the rights of Pharaoh could not be enforced, for the fields of grain and the pastures were destroyed,

32 the highborn and the lowly prayed together that life might come to an end! and the turmoil and thundering cease to beat upon their ears!

33 terror was the companion of men by day! and horror their companion by night!

34 men lost their senses and became mad! they were distracted by frightfulness!

35 on the great night of the Destroyer's wrath, when it's terror was at its height, there was a hail of rocks, and the Earth heaved as pain rent her bowels!

36 gates, columns, and walls were consumed by fire, and the statues of elohim were overthrown and broken,

37 the people who fled outside their dwellings in fear were slain by the hail, and those who took shelter from the hail were swallowed when the Earth split open!

38 the habitations of men collapsed upon those inside, and there was panic on every hand!

39 the land burnt like tinder!

40 as those watched upon their rooftops, the Heavens hurled wrath upon them and they died!

41 the land writhed under the wrath of the Destroyer! and groaned with the agony of Egypt!

42 it shook itself, and the temples and palaces of the nobles were thrown down from their foundations,

43 the highborn ones perished in the midst of the ruins, and all the strength of the land was stricken,

44 even the great one, the first born of Pharaoh, died with the

highborn in the midst of the terror and falling stones,

45 the children of princes were cast out into the streets, and those who were not cast out died within their abodes!

46 there were nine days of darkness and upheaval, while a tempest raged such as never had been known before,

47 but the slaves, who lived in huts in the reedlands, at the place of pits, were spared!

Chapter 6c

1 The people were weak from fear and bestowed gold, silver, lapis lazuli, turquoise, and copper upon the slaves, and to their priests they gave chalices, urns, and ornaments,

2 as the slaves spared by the Destroyer left the accursed land forthwith,

3 their multitude moved in the gloom of a half dawn, under a mantle of fine swirling grey ash, leaving the burnt fields and shattered cities behind them,

4 many Egyptians attached themselves to the host, for one who was great led them forth, a priest-prince of the inner courtyard,

5 fire mounted up on high! and its burning left with the enemies of Egypt, it rose up from the ground as a fountain, and hung as a curtain in the sky!

6 in seven days they journeyed to the waters, they crossed the heaving wilderness while the hills melted around them! and above, the skies were torn with lightning,

7 they were sped by terror, but their feet became entangled in the land and the wilderness shut them in, they knew not the way, for no sign was constant before them,

8 they turned before Noshari and stopped at Shokoth, the place of quarries, they passed the waters of Maha and came by the valley of Pikaroth, northward of Mara they came up against the waters which blocked their way, and their hearts were in despair,

9 that night was a night of fear and dread! for there was a high moaning above, and black winds from the underworld were loosed as fire sprang up from the ground!

10 the hearts of the slaves shrank within them, for they knew the wrath of Pharaoh followed them and that there was no way of escape,

11 they hurled abuse on those who led them! the slaves disputed among themselves, and there was violence! selah;

12 Pharaoh had gathered his army and followed the slaves; after he departed, there were riots and disorders behind him, for the cities were plundered,

13 the torot were cast out of the judgment halls and trampled underfoot in the streets,

14 the storehouses and granaries were burst open and robbed, roads were flooded and none could pass along them, people lay dead on every side,

15 the palace was split, and the princes and officials fled, so that none was left with authority to command,

16 the lists of numbers were destroyed, public places were overthrown, and households became confused and unknown;

17 the host of Pharaoh came upon the slaves by the saltwater shores, but was held back from them by a breath of fire!

18 a great cloud was spread over the hosts and darkened the sky,

19 none could see, except for the fiery glow and the unceasing lightnings, which rent the covering cloud overhead,

20 a whirlwind arose in the east and swept over the encamped hosts, a gale raged all night, and in the red, twilit dawn, there was a movement of the Earth, the waters receded from the seashore, and were rolled back on themselves!

21 there was a strange silence, and then, in the gloom, it was seen that the waters had parted, leaving a passage between!

22 the land had risen, but it was disturbed and trembled, the way was not straight or clear,

23 the waters about were as if spun within a bowl, the swampland alone remained undisturbed,

24 suddenly, from the horn of the Destroyer came a high, shrilling noise, which stopped the ears of men!

25 the slaves had been making sacrifices in despair, their lamentations were loud,

26 now, before the strange sound, there was hesitation and doubt, for the space of a breath all stood still and silent,

27 then, all was confusion and shouting! some pressing forward into the waters, against all who sought to flee back from the unstable ground,

28 then in exaltation, their leader led them into the midst of the waters through the confusion! yet, many sought to turn back into the host behind them, while others fled along the empty shores!

29 then, all became still over the sea and upon the shore, as behind, the Earth shook, and boulders split with a great noise!

30 the wrath of Heaven was removed to a distance, and stood upwards of the two hosts,

31 stern faces were lit darkly by the fiery curtain, then, the fury departed, and there was silence,

32 stillness spread over the land while the host of Pharaoh stood without movement in the red glow,

33 the curtain of fire rolled up into a dark billowing cloud, which spread out as a canopy,

34 then with a shout, the captains went forward! and the host rose up behind them!

35 there was a stirring of the waters,

36 they followed them past the place of the great whirlpool,

37 the passage was confused in the midst of the waters and the ground beneath unstable,

38 then the stillness was broken by a mighty roar! and through the rolling pillars of cloud, the wrath of the Destroyer descended upon the hosts!

39 the Heavens roared as with a thousand thunders!

40 the bowels of the Earth were sundered! and Earth shrieked its

agony!

41 the cliffs were torn away and cast down, the dry ground fell beneath the waters, and great waves broke upon the shore, sweeping in rocks from seaward!

42 the great surge of rocks and waters overwhelmed the chariots of the Egyptians who went before the footmen,

43 and the chariot of the Pharaoh was hurled into the air, as if by a mighty hand, and was crushed in the midst of the rolling waters!

Chapter 6d

1 Tidings of the disaster came back by Rageb, son of Thomat, who hastened on ahead of the terrified survivors because of his burning,

2 he brought reports unto the people that the host had been destroyed by blast and deluge, the captains had gone, the strong men had fallen, and none remained to command!

3 therefore because of the calamities which had befallen them, the people revolted,

4 cowards slunk from their lairs and came forth boldly to assume the high offices of the dead,

5 comely and noble women, their protectors gone, were prey,

6 the broken land lay helpless, and invaders came out of the gloom like carrion,

7 a strange people came up against Egypt, and none stood to fight, for strength and courage were gone,

8 the invaders came up out of the land because of the wrath of Heaven which had laid their own land waste,

9 there, too, had been a plague of reptiles and ants, signs and omens and an earthquake!

10 there, also, had been turmoil and disaster, disorder and famine, with the grey breath of the Destroyer sweeping the ground and stopping the breath of men!

11 deserted by the elohim above and below, their dwellings destroyed, their households scattered, they were as men already half dead,

12 their hearts were still filled with terror, and with the memory of the wrath which had struck them from out of Heaven,

13 they were still filled with the memory of the fearsome sight of the Destroyer, and they knew not what they did!

14 when it passed away, brother buried brother throughout the land,

15 men rose up against those in authority, and fled from the cities to dwell in tents in the outlands;

16 Egypt lacked great men to deal with the times;

17 but good times came again, even under the invaders, and ships sailed upstream!

18 the air was purified, the breath of the Destroyer passed away, and the land became filled again with growing things!

19 life was renewed throughout the whole land!

Chapter 7

1 This is the Doomshape, called the Destroyer in Egypt, and all
the lands thereabouts:

2 In colour, it was bright and fiery,

3 in appearance, changing and unstable,

4 it twisted about itself like a coil, like water bubbling into a pool
from an underground supply, and all men agree it was a most
fearsome sight!

5 it was not a great comet or a loosened star, being more like a
fiery body of flame,

6 its movements on high were slow,

7 below it swirled in the manner of smoke, and it remained close
to the sun, whose face it hid,

8 there was a bloody redness about it, which changed as it passed
along its course,

9 it caused death and destruction in its rising and setting,

10 it swept the Earth with grey cinder rain and caused many
plagues, hunger, and other evils!

11 it bit the skin of men and beast until they became mottled with
sores,

12 the Earth was troubled and shook, the hills and mountains
moved and rocked!

13 the dark smoke-filled Heavens bowed over Earth, and a great howl came to the ears of living men, borne to them upon the wings of the wind,

14 it was the cry of the Doomshape! The Master of Dread!

15 thick clouds of fiery smoke passed before him, and there was an awful hail of hot stones and coals of fire!

16 the Doomshape thundered sharply in the Heavens and shot out bright lightnings,

17 the channels of water were turned back unto themselves when the land tilted, and great trees were tossed about and snapped like twigs,

18 then, a voice like ten thousand trumpets was heard over the wilderness, and before its burning breath, the flames parted,

19 the whole of the land moved and mountains melted! the sky itself roared like ten thousand lions in agony, and bright arrows of blood sped back and forth across its face!

20 the Earth swelled up like bread upon the hearth!

21 this was the aspect of the Doomshape, called the Destroyer, when it appeared in days long gone by, in olden times, it is thus described in the old records, few of which remain,

22 it is said that when it appears in the Heavens above, Earth splits open from the heat, like a nut roasted before the fire,

23 then, flames shoot up through the surface and leap about like fiery fiends upon the fallen black blood,

24 the moisture inside the land is all dried up, the pastures and cultivated places are consumed in flames, and they and all trees become white ashes!

25 the Doomshape is like a circling ball of flame, which scatters small fiery offspring in its train,

26 it covers about a fifth part of the sky, and sends writhing snakelike fingers down to Earth,

27 before it, the sky appears frightened, and it breaks up and scatters away,

28 midday is no brighter than night, and it spawns a host of terrible things!

29 in the days of visitation, do not pray that the El of Judgment be on your side, pray rather, that you be on the side of the El of Judgment!

30 these are things said of the Destroyer in the old records, though they speak of things in the past, they tell of things to come,

31 read them with solemn heart, knowing that the Doomshape has its appointed time and will return,

32 it would be foolish to let them go unheeded!

33 now, men say, "Such things are not destined for our days!" may the Great Adonai Above grant that this be so!

34 but, come the day surely will, and in accordance with his nature, man will be unprepared.

The Lived Religion - Book 12 - Prayer

Chapter 1

1 True Elohim, by Whom the worthy are guided in all they undertake, Who rises as a beacon in the darkness for the lowly,

2 grant us, Your servants who put their trust in You, strength to overcome all the doubts and uncertainties, which rise in our hearts, like frightening shadows arising in the night,

3 let us sip the waters from the inexhaustible well of wisdom,

4 that we may not move along false paths to bring about our own destruction! for we cannot see the way in the enveloping darkness,

5 confusing voices shout this way or that, and we are bewildered, for we know not which one is right!

6 we are not men of great learning or high position,

7 we do not sit among princes, being among the lowliest in the land, yet it is we who carry the burdens of the people,

8 we feed the hungry and provide for the widow and orphan, ours are the aching backs and weary feet, ours the naked body and empty bowl!

9 those who are concerned with higher things sit at tables of bounty, those seemingly unworthy rejoice amid prosperity and plenty,

10 those who take are given more, while those who give are mocked,

11 we cannot ask to win, but we can ask to be made strong, if we struggle for strength!

12 we cannot ask to remain unhurt, but we do ask for courage, as we fight!

13 we cannot ask to be supported in weakness, but we can ask for the fortitude to endure!

14 we stand firm-footed, grim-faced to the foe!

15 the forces of wickedness encompass us about, but we will surge forward with closed ranks until we come to shabbat in the presence of Victory!

16 O Adon, Supreme Among Elohim, watch over us in the struggle, for we are Your children!

Chapter 2

1 According to Your Kodesh Word, my duty is to always protect those who walk with me and never deny my beliefs,

2 I shall be steadfast even under persecution, the tormentors' instruments will not open my mouth,

3 I undertake to bring at least one convert into the light,

4 I will not wilfully harm a wild creature or life of a plant,

5 my duty is to oppose all forms of disorder and torah-lessness,

6 it is to learn the purpose of life, and to try to understand the Design of The Supreme Elohim, Who laid all things out in

orderliness,

7 I know I must always keep my thoughts clean, my words true and good, and my deeds manly,

8 I know there is a path of evil: It is the way of weakness and cowardice, which leads to self-destruction!

9 I will fight all forms of wickedness and evil, wherever I find them, and I know I cannot go manfully through life without opposition and struggle,

10 I know that all men are born mortal and all must die in body, but I believe I am a soul, with the potential of everlasting life!

11 if during the trials of life I am assailed by doubt, I will not remain passive before it!

12 I will never oppress any man for his belief, unless he first attack mine, even then, I will bear him with tolerance, until his oppression threatens to overwhelm me,

13 I will never agree to the conversion of men by force, even for their own good, for this is an evil thing,

14 my only arguments shall be example and common sense!

15 the faith I hold shall not be something imprisoned within my thoughts, but a Lived Religion, one expressed in deeds!

16 I give thanks for the knowledge that I am a living soul, but I know full well the grave responsibility I bear towards my future being!

17 I will not be a disgrace to Earth when I pass to the Greater Realm beyond!

18 I recognise that my soul and body compete for the satisfaction of their separate desires,

19 I know that each day the body dies a little, that every day it draws nearer to the dark shore,

20 therefore, I will follow the precepts of prudence, and each and every day will be a step forward in the awakening of my soul!

21 I shall not punish my true self for the sake of satisfying a decaying body.

Chapter 3

1 Supreme One, illuminate the hearts of Your people! and let them see the way ahead!

2 permit them to understand the meaning of life,

3 make their hearts fearful for the responsibility they carry with regard to the future state of their souls, to this end, help them towards achieving a humble ruach and a kindly heart,

4 grant them some glimpse of Eternity while here on Earth, so that they may better understand what lies before them,

5 bestow upon them the ability to make contact with the Fount of Wisdom and Truth, and let them draw near the Well of Holiness to sip its waters,

6 help them to make right judgments and guide their hearts, so they hold fast to the teachings which have gone before,

7 make them steadfast in the light, and, show them the falsity that

glitters in the darkness,

8 when they come to the end of their journey, Supreme One, grant them immortality in the Region of Eternal Light!

9 incline towards them in mercy, for You can even mitigate the impress of wickedness upon their everlasting souls!

10 indeed, Supreme One, I have brought about much sorrow and suffering in my days, the burden of my manhood has weighed down heavily upon me,

11 but, O Supreme Elohim, I have never robbed the widow or fatherless, or struck at the helpless and those without protection,

12 I have not mocked the afflicted, or stood aside in fear when wickedness was being done,

13 I have slain no man,

14 when I served any man, I served him well,

15 I have never deserted a friend in distress, or violated the sanctity of another man's home,

16 yet, Supreme One, in my life I have done much else to be condemned, and therefore, cannot know my standing before You,

17 Almighty Abba, I cannot say, as others do, that I have no doubts, for indeed I am often torn with conflicting thoughts,

18 I do not doubt Your existence, for I have been granted a manifestation of its reality,

19 but I am full of doubts about my relationship with You!

20 then, too, there is so much I cannot understand, yet others turn to me for guidance,

21 when I make an error affecting only myself, I do not complain about the consequences, but should I guide others into error, my heart will be torn apart!

22 Adonai of My Heart and Abba of My Soul, incline towards me a little! for of myself I cannot reach You!

23 enlighten me, so that I may lead others into the light!

24 however I stand in Your eyes, do not consider me too unworthy to plead for Your people!

25 guide me, Supreme One, what shall I do for Your people?

26 death and destruction I do not fear, not even everlasting nothingness, but I do fear being inadequate for my task,

27 Supreme One, give me confidence and strength! I ask no more, if I cannot find these with You, I can find them nowhere.

Chapter 4

1 Amid my youth, O Creator, You seemed close, yet I could not understand You, for the teachings of others wished to enclose You in a box,

2 now, though You appear further away, I see more clearly, and have glimpsed Your nature,

3 when I could not understand You in one place, I sought You in another,

4 I looked for You where there was more light!

5 O Great One, hidden within the Eternal Silence, shining as a beacon of pure light to men! lighten our darkness and our fear-shadowed hearts!

6 lift the veil just slightly, that we may understand something of Your greatness!

7 we are not uninstructed, and know we can be granted no more than a glimpse of Your Glory, for to receive more would be too awesome for the frail constitution of man,

8 this is why the ignorant doubt, for their very ignorance spawns the frailty which inhibits their enlightenment!

9 O Great One, grant that the ruach within us may be helped to cleanse itself of the besmirching foulness spawned by our thoughts,

10 remove from us every trace of that which may pollute, and let us know Timeless Splendour in glory!

11 many great men have praised You in error, not knowing what was good for them, they sought to attain the things which fed the flesh alone,

12 O Great One, show such as these the error of their ways, giving them not the good things of life unworthily,

13 but make them better men that they may be worthy of their blessings,

14 You have loved us with an exceedingly great love! having compassion on our many failings and weaknesses, knowing that men are but frail creatures prone to go astray,

15 O El of Elohim, for the sake of our fathers who placed their trust in You, to whom You gave the Mitsvahs of Life, be merciful to us!

16 instruct and guide us along the paths we should follow,

17 lead us through the many entanglements of earthly life, so we may finally come to shabbat in Your safekeeping!

18 when the sky blushes in the dawning I will lift up my voice in gladness! and when it reddens in the evening I will not remain silent!

19 I will pluck strings and send sweet musical sounds rising to my Adon! and my breath will fill pipes with tunes to His Glory!

20 I will raise my voice! and my hands will move with the music!

21 the season of first gathering to the full time of harvest, the season of sowing to the season of fruitfulness, all pass away as the kiss of the wind on the waters,

22 the Decrees of Adonai are fulfilled in the moadim, and the days of labour pass one into the other;

23 I will be joyful in the fullness of ruach! at the beginning and at the end of the moadim I will rejoice, and sing songs of praise with a full heart!

24 and I will shun the hypocrisy of those with moving lips;

25 O Great One, protect me! O Abba, save me! hear the words of my heart!

26 I was one who tried to be ever mindful of what was right and

what was wrong,

27 I chose what I thought was right, and shunned that which I thought was wrong,

28 I listened to those who were wiser than I, and helped those who were less privileged, can man do more?

29 may you, my friends, find Eternal springs of strength and courage welling up in your souls at the time of your testing!

30 we, your brothers, go our destined way, and we shall not likely meet again in this earthly likeness,

31 may your future amid the Fountain of Light be glorious and beautiful!

32 and may you span the great gulf of the Eternal years in splendour of form and ruach!

33 I commend you to the care of the Great Adonai, may He protect you and keep you from evil.

www.ingramcontent.com/pod-product-compliance
Lightning Source LLC
Chambersburg PA
CBHW060411130626
46555CB00005B/2029